D1592459

written and illustrated by

SUSAN PURDY

CHRISTMAS
GIFTS
GOOD
ENOUGH
TO EAT!

A Holiday Cookbook

FRANKLIN WATTS
New York / London /
Toronto / Sydney
1981

A GROLIER COMPANY

Library of Congress Cataloging in Publication Data
Purdy, Susan Gold
Christmas gifts good enough to eat.
(A Holiday cookbook)
Includes index.
SUMMARY: Includes simple step-by step recipes
for candies, cakes, breads, snacks, sauces, and
cheeses suitable to give as holiday gifts.
1.   Christmas cookery—Juvenile literature.
2.   Cookery—Juvenile literature.
3.   Gifts—Juvenile literature.
[1.   Christmas cookery. 2.   Cookery.
3.   Gifts] I. Title.
TX739.P83   641.5′68   80–28510
ISBN 0–531–03542–5
ISBN 0–531–04314–2 (lib. bdg.)

CHRISTMAS GIFTS GOOD ENOUGH TO EAT

Also by Susan Purdy:

CHRISTMAS COOKBOOK
HALLOWEEN COOKBOOK
JEWISH HOLIDAY COOKBOOK

Here is a giant birthday cookie for David Apple

For help and encouragement in preparing this collection of recipes, I especially want to thank my family, Geoffrey and Cassandra Purdy, Nancy and David Lieberman, and Frances Joslin Gold, as well as my students (both adults and children) at the Silo Cooking School in New Milford, Connecticut, my young cooking students at the Montessori School in Washington, Connecticut, and my many friends who helped test and taste.

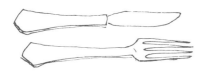 Contents

A Gift from My Kitchen to Yours

A homemade gift from your kitchen is a double gift—twice as good as a store-bought one—for besides tasting much better, the time, thought, and effort of the cook is appreciated, too. A gift from your kitchen is a gift of love, and you can be sure those who receive it will enjoy eating it as much as you enjoyed making it.

The recipes in this collection include some that are quick and easy to make for last-minute gifts, some that you can make well ahead of the holidays and freeze or store, and some that are more complex and require time to prepare. Please read the introductory GIFT NOTE before each recipe so you will understand what is involved and know how to plan your time and gift presentation. For packing, wrapping, and mailing food gifts, please read the following notes.

Susan Purdy
1981

How to Package Food Gifts

1. Containers: Look for readily available containers that can be recycled. Also look for unusual containers to fill with food gifts, making two gifts in one.

Most cookies and candies stay fresh best in airtight containers; good ones are wide-mouth jars with lids, plastic freezer boxes, metal tins, or coffee cans with snap-on lids. You can make attractive packages with cardboard boxes (when they are cleaned and decorated), round cereal boxes, or even egg cartons (for candies wrapped first in plastic wrap).

For an especially elegant gift, try packing cookies first in a plastic bag; then set them in a pretty basket lined with a checkered napkin. Pack candies in apothecary jars or brandy snifters (sealed with plastic wrap and tied with a bow), and put cakes on a new baking pan. Flour or sugar canisters will hold a large quantity of crackers, cookies, or pretzels, as will clay flowerpots. Extra-large sugar scoops, wooden cheese boards, bread trays, salad bowls, tin or copper dessert molds, soufflé dishes, mixing bowls, saucepans, even frying pans all make containers for homemade food gifts. Alongside the bow and recipe, tie on a wooden spoon or fancy cookie cutter for a bonus gift.

2. Labels: Don't forget to label food gifts with recipe name and how or when to serve it. Add your own name and date. Use self-sticking or taped-on labels. Don't forget to label those foods that need refrigeration. Labeling directions precede each recipe in this book.

3. Recipe tags: Write recipes on small index cards, adding your name and date. Punch a hole in card and tie on package.

HOW TO DECORATE FOOD PACKAGES

Jars:

Use "mason" or preserving jars, or recycled jars with lids (soak to remove label, wash and dry). You can draw on the jars with oil-base felt pens or china-markers, or decorate them with cutouts of colored tape or self-stick seals and stars.

FABRIC   PAPER   DOILY

Lids:

Cover jar or box lids with plain self-sticking mailing labels, or glued-on colored paper, tape, fabric, or felt. Attach bows on lids with an inside-out roll of tape. Paper doilies can be glued flat on lids or gathered into pompons by pinching in at the center; fold center over and tape to lid.

See-Through Wrap:

Most foods look too pretty to cover with gift wrapping paper. Instead, set the gift on a plate (paper, tin, china, or cut from cardboard) and cover it with a double thickness of clear plastic, overlapping the ends to preserve freshness. Tie with a colored ribbon and add tag. Also add recipe if you like.

Cans and Boxes:

Coffee cans with plastic lids are great cookie jars when decorated with glued-on colored paper (or pressed on self-adhesive Contac paper). Use felt pens, crayons, or colored tape to decorate sides. Boxes can be decorated in the same way and, for a permanent finish, sprayed (away from food!) with shellac or urethane glaze. Milk cartons can also be used for containers, provided they are washed thoroughly and have no lingering milk odor.

Oddly Shaped Packages:

Wrap them in colored or brown paper bags decorated with your own designs and tied with ribbons. Or, give an extra gift by wrapping unevenly shaped containers in squares of brightly colored fabric or large cloth napkins or dish towels.

HOW TO MAIL FOOD PACKAGES

Wrapping:

Your post office will give you advice and special booklets about regulations for mailing all types of packages, including foods. In general, small packages and fragile items like cookies should be wrapped individually in paper, then set in cushioning material (styrofoam chips, bubble wrap, or unbuttered popcorn) within a stronger carton. Or, you may wrap cookies or candies individually, cushion them in their own box, then set them in a second, stronger carton with cushioning material between the two, so that the inner box cannot slide around.

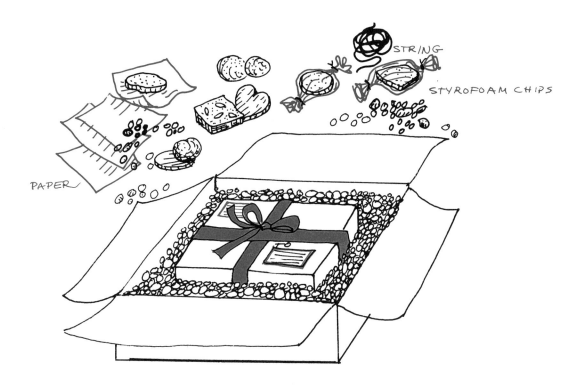

Sealing Packages:

Use reinforced tape—with fiber filaments—to close cartons. Masking or cellophane tape is too weak and should not be used; string is likely to get caught in postal processing machines.

Labeling Packages:

Put one address label inside the package (just in case the outside label comes off or gets blurred) and, of course, a second address label on the outside of the carton. Be sure it is well taped or glued down. Use waterproof ink.

Special mailing instructions for the post office should be marked on cartons three times: above the address, below the postage, and on the back of the carton. Mark FRAGILE—if contents could break; PERISHABLE—if foods could spoil.

Postage:

For quick delivery, food gifts should be mailed *First Class* or *Priority Mail.* Ask your postmaster for details.

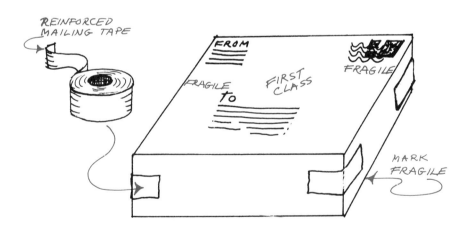

Before You Begin

If the arrangement of these recipes looks different to you, it is. In most recipes, ingredients are listed first, then you are told what to do with them. I have told you what foods to get ready, then listed ingredients and instructions when and where you actually use them. My testers find this method always works; I hope you will agree. I also hope you will have the patience to read all the way through a recipe before starting it. This will help you plan your time as well as your activities.

If you plan to use the metric measurements in this book (they are placed alongside the standard measurements), be sure to read the introductory note on Measurements. If you use the standard measurements, proceed as you ordinarily would.

1. Safety: Keep pot handles turned away from the stove front so pots will not be bumped into and spilled. Turn off oven or stove-top as soon as you are through using it. When pots are removed from stove, place them on a heat-proof surface. To prevent fires, keep potholders, dishtowels, aprons, and your clothes away from stove burners. Keep a fire extinguisher in the kitchen just in case (and learn how to use it).

To prevent accidental cuts, store and wash knives separately from other utensils. Only use blender or food processor with an adult's supervision or permission.

2. Butter: All butter used for the recipes in this book is lightly salted unless otherwise noted, when the recipe will say "sweet" butter. Margarine can almost always be substituted for butter, and in most recipes both are listed. In recipes that taste much better made with butter, margarine has been left off the ingredients list.

3. Flour: For better nutrition, use *unbleached* all-purpose flour instead of bleached. You will find the word *unbleached* on the front of the flour package. Flour is not sifted unless the recipe specifically calls for it. To sift flour, see Basic Skills.

4. Sugar: Sugar is not sifted unless the recipe specifically calls for it. Turbinado (unrefined) sugar can be substituted for an equal amount of granulated white sugar. To substitute honey for granulated sugar, use about ⅞ as much (1 cup sugar = 250 ml = ⅞ cup honey = 220 ml) *and* use about 3 tablespoons (45 ml) *less* liquid in recipe.

5. Eggs: All eggs used in recipes are large size.

6. Wheat germ: To increase nutritional value of recipes, we have added wheat germ wherever possible. We generally prefer to use unflavored toasted wheat germ, but raw unflavored wheat germ may be substituted.

7. Other health-food substitutions: To increase nutritional value of recipes, you can substitute 1 tablespoon (15 ml) sifted soy flour *plus* 1 tablespoon (15 ml) powdered dry milk *plus* 1 tablespoon (15 ml) wheat germ for an equal amount of flour in all cookie and cake recipes. NOTE: Soy flour causes quicker browning, so if you use it, lower oven temperature about 25°.

8. The timer: Whenever a recipe gives two times (such as 10 to 12 minutes), set your timer for the first time (10). Test for doneness. If necessary, reset timer for additional time (2 minutes) and cook longer.

9. Oven heat: Oven temperatures vary. It is very rare for the actual temperature inside the oven to be exactly the same as the one you set on the thermostat dial. If your foods do not cook in the time or manner described in the recipe, it may be because your oven is too hot, or not as hot as the heat indicated by your thermostat. To be safe, use a separate oven thermometer (sold in a hardware store) that hangs or sits on the oven shelf. Change the temperature on your outside thermostat dial until the inside oven temperature is correct.

Measurements: Standard and Metric

This book is designed to be used EITHER with standard measurements OR with metric measurements. In each recipe, you will see both units listed side by side—for example, 1 cup flour (250 ml; 165 g). Select one method and use it consistently. If you choose to cook with the standard method, use the recipes as you ordinarily would, with standard measuring cups and spoons, and ignore the numbers in the parentheses. If you choose the metric system, don't convert, just cook! All the measurements you need are in the parentheses beside each ingredient; ignore the standard cup and spoon measurements. Use metric utensils or the widely available ones with markings in both standard and metric units.

These utensils have milliliter markings that are rounded off to the nearest useful whole units. Thus, 1 cup is usually marked 250 ml. You should be aware that this is an approximation. Do not try to figure out apparent irregularities, just use the measurements as they are in this book. All our recipes have been tested with the metric quantities listed, and they work. We have also rounded off our metric quantities to their nearest useful whole units whenever possible.

Practical Examples

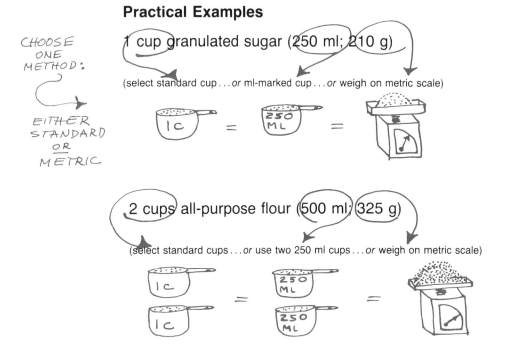

CHOOSE ONE METHOD:

EITHER STANDARD OR METRIC

1 cup granulated sugar (250 ml; 210 g)

(select standard cup...or ml-marked cup...or weigh on metric scale)

1 C = 250 ML =

2 cups all-purpose flour (500 ml; 325 g)

(select standard cups...or use two 250 ml cups...or weigh on metric scale)

1 C / 1 C = 250 ML / 250 ML =

Basic Skills

To Level Measurements:

All measurements in this book are level unless otherwise specified. To level a measuring cup or spoon, fill it until slightly mounded, then draw the back of a knife blade over the top, scraping the surface flat.

To Measure Butter or Shortening:

Butter or margarine is easiest to measure when purchased in quarter-pound sticks.

1 pound	= 4 sticks	= 2 cups	= 480 ml	= 480 g
1 stick	= ½ cup	= 8 tablespoons	= 120 ml	= 120 g

Instead of measuring by the stick, you can pack the butter down very firmly into a measuring cup (be sure there are no air spaces trapped in the bottom), or you can use the "water displacement" method: To measure ¼ cup (60 ml) butter, fill a 1-cup (250 ml) measuring cup ¾ full (185 ml) with cold water. Add pieces of butter until the water reaches the 1-cup (250 ml) mark. Pour off water and you are left with ¼ cup (60 ml) measured butter.

To Sift Flour:

Sifting lightens the texture of baked goods. You can use either a strainer or a sifter for this process. Flour is sifted only where the recipe specifically calls for it.

Sift the required amount of flour onto a sheet of wax paper. Then pick up the paper, pull the edges around into a sort of funnel, and *gently* pour as much flour as you need back into a measuring cup. You can also use a spoon to transfer flour. Do not shake or pack measured flour. Level top of cup with knife blade, then add flour to recipe. Or return re-measured flour to sifter, add other dry ingredients, such as baking powder and salt, and sift everything together into the other ingredients in recipe.

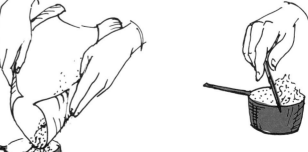

To Weigh Flour:

Sift flour onto a piece of wax paper as explained above. Then spoon sifted flour lightly onto your wax-paper-lined scale until the measure is correct.

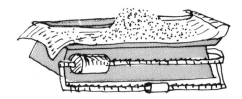

To Roll Out Dough:

There are two ways to roll out dough. One is on a countertop or a pastry board, the other between sheets of wax paper. If you are using a countertop or a pastry board, spread it lightly with flour so the dough will not stick. Also flour the rolling pin. Then roll out the dough, adding more flour if dough sticks. Some pastry boards and rolling pins are covered with cotton cloth (called a sock) to help prevent sticking; cloths should also be floured.

The second method is to cut two pieces of wax paper, each roughly 14" (36 cm) long. Place one piece flat on the counter and flour it lightly. Place dough on floured paper, then sprinkle a little flour on top of dough. Cover dough with second paper. Use rolling pin (unfloured) to roll out dough between the papers. Peel the paper off and put it back on again if it gets too wrinkled. When dough is correct thickness, peel top paper off dough.

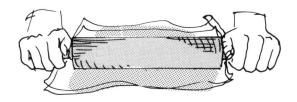

To Separate an Egg:

Here are two different ways to separate an egg. The first method may be new to you, but try it anyway. It is very easy, never breaks the yolk, and is a lot of fun.

First wash your hands, as you will be touching the egg. Crack egg in half by tapping it sharply against side of bowl. Hold egg on its side as shown, grasping ends with your fingers. Fit tips of thumbs into crack. Pull shells apart and *at the same time* turn one half shell upright so it contains all the egg. Hold this shell, containing egg, upright with one hand while the other hand discards the empty half shell. Then turn empty hand palm up, fingers together, over a clean dry bowl. Pour out the entire egg onto the fingers of the empty hand. Spread fingers apart very slightly to let the egg white drip between them into the bowl while the yolk rests on top of the fingers as shown. Collect all of the white in a bowl; put yolk in a separate bowl.

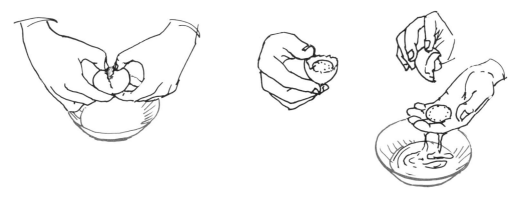

The most common procedure is to break egg in half, then hold half shell containing the yolk upright in one hand while you pour the egg white from the other half shell into a bowl. Then tip yolk out into the empty shell while white that surrounded it falls into bowl below. Place yolk in separate bowl.

Cookies

GINGERBREAD CHRISTMAS CARDS

A new idea for gingerbread cookies: cut them into oversized cards and write your greetings with frosting.

GIFT NOTE: To give a cookie card as a gift, wrap it in protective tissue and place in a box. To mail cookie cards, roll the dough a good ¼" (.5 cm) thick so cookies are not too fragile. Wrap cards carefully, then cushion well with styrofoam or popcorn (see page 12 for mailing directions) before packing in a carton (not an envelope).

Card cookies can also be hung on the Christmas tree; before baking, poke each cookie with a hole for a string.

EQUIPMENT:
Measuring cups and spoons
Small saucepan
Cookie sheet
Rubber scraper
2 large mixing bowls
Electric mixer *or* whisk
Mixing spoon
Wax paper and plastic wrap
Rolling pin
Paring knife *or* table knife
Pencil
Ruler
Scissors
Cardboard 4" × 6" (10 × 15 cm)
Wide-bladed pancake turner
Wire rack
Frosting decorating tube—optional

FOODS YOU WILL NEED:
Dough:
½ cup (1 stick) margarine (125 ml; 120 g)
½ cup granulated sugar (125 ml; 105 g)
½ cup molasses (preferably unsulfured type; 125 ml)
2¼ cups all-purpose flour (560 ml; 365 g)
½ teaspoon baking soda (2.5 ml)
½ teaspoon salt (2.5 ml)
Spices:
½ teaspoon nutmeg (2.5 ml)
½ teaspoon cinnamon (2.5 ml)
1½ teaspoons ground ginger (7.5 ml)

DECORATIVE ICING:
1 tablespoon lemon juice (15 ml)
1 egg white
1¾ cups confectioners' sugar (435 ml; 215 g)
Pinch of cream of tartar
Pinch of salt

Ingredients:

(To make 6 cards each 4″ × 6″ [10 × 15 cm] or about 20 cookie cutter shapes)

½ cup (1 stick) margarine (125 ml; 120 g)

½ cup granulated sugar (125 ml; 105 g)
½ cup molasses (125 ml)

2 cups all-purpose flour (500 ml; 325 g)
½ teaspoon baking soda (2.5 ml)
½ teaspoon salt (2.5 ml)
Spices:
½ teaspoon nutmeg (2.5 ml)
½ teaspoon cinnamon (2.5 ml)
1½ teaspoons ground ginger (7.5 ml)

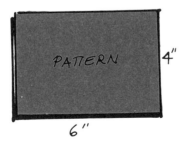

PATTERN   4″

6″

How To:

1. Turn oven on to 350° F (175° C). Measure margarine into small pan and set on stove over low heat. When melted, use rubber scraper to scoop margarine into large mixing bowl.

2. Add sugar and molasses to melted margarine and beat well.

3. Add flour, baking soda, salt, and spices to sugar-margarine mixture and stir slowly until blended. Beat until dough forms a ball. If dough feels too soft to shape, add a little more flour. Gather dough into a ball and set out on a lightly floured work surface. Knead dough a few times by pushing on it with the heels of your hands. Roll dough up in wax paper and refrigerate while making card pattern.

4. Draw, then cut out a rectangular cardboard pattern about 4″ × 6″ (10 × 15 cm) or whatever size you prefer for your card.

5. Remove dough from refrigerator. Divide dough roughly in half and roll out one part at a time directly on *ungreased* cookie

sheet. Cover rolling pin with cloth or lightly flour it to keep dough from sticking. Roll dough about ¼" (.5 cm) thick for cards. (You can also use cookie cutters to make shapes.)

6. Place card pattern on rolled dough and cut around edges with knife point. Peel away scraps. Scraps can be molded into bits of trim, moistened underneath with a drop of water, and pressed onto card edges. Be sure to leave center area free for writing.

7. Place cookie sheet in preheated 350° F (175° C) oven and set timer to bake 10 to 13 minutes, or until cookies are firm and edges are just slightly darker color than middle. Remove from oven with potholders. Cool cookies on baking sheet. With wide pancake turner, gently transfer cookies to wire rack for decorating.

Decorative Icing:

1 tablespoon lemon juice (15 ml)
1 egg white
1¾ cups confectioners' sugar (435 ml; 215 g)
Pinch of cream of tartar
Pinch of salt

1. In mixing bowl, combine lemon juice and egg white. Sift in confectioners' sugar. Add pinch of cream of tartar and salt.

2. Beat until smooth. Mixture should be like softly whipped cream. Add a little more sugar if too thin, more juice if too thick. Until ready to use, cover icing with plastic wrap so it stays soft.

3. Put icing into decorating tube (or make your own from wax paper, see page 49). Decorate cookies. Let icing harden before wrapping.

SWEDISH FINGER COOKIES

Melt-in-your-mouth almond cookies, *Mördegspinnar* are everyone's favorites: easy to make and irresistible.

GIFT NOTE: Finger cookies can be made ahead and frozen. They remain crisp when packaged in an airtight container. Finger cookies can be mailed, but are fragile and may break.

EQUIPMENT:
Cookie sheet
Measuring cups and spoons
Blender *or* food processor *or* nut grinder
Mixing bowl
Electric mixer *or* spoon
Sifter
Plate
Wax paper
Wire rack
Spatula

FOODS YOU WILL NEED:
1 cup almonds, either with skins on *or* blanched (250 ml; 135 g)
1 teaspoon vanilla extract (5 ml)
1 cup (2 sticks) sweet butter (250 ml; 240 g), at room temperature
¼ cup plus 1¾ cups confectioners' sugar (500 ml; 250 g)
2 cups all-purpose flour (500 ml; 325 g)

Ingredients:

How To:

(To make 100 cookies)

1 cup almonds, either with skins on *or* blanched (250 ml; 135 g)

1 teaspoon vanilla extract (5 ml)
1 cup (2 sticks) sweet butter (250 ml; 240 g), at room temperature
¼ cup confectioners' sugar (60 ml; 30 g)
2 cups all-purpose flour (500 ml; 325 g)

1. Grease cookie sheet with wrapper from butter package. Grind nuts finely, a few at a time, in blender *or* food processor *or* nut grinder. Put nuts in mixing bowl.

2. Add the vanilla extract and the butter, broken up in small pieces. Sift in ¼ cup (60 ml) confectioners' sugar and mix well. Then add flour slowly, beating until well combined. Dough should form a ball. Turn oven on to 350° F (175° C).

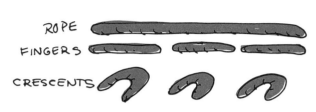

ROPE
FINGERS
CRESCENTS

1¾ cups confectioners' sugar (435 ml; 220 g)

3. Wash hands, as you will be handling dough. Flour hands lightly. Break off walnut-sized lumps of dough and roll them into ropes about the thickness of your finger. Break or cut ropes into finger-length sections and set them on greased cookie sheet. Ropes can be left straight or bent into crescents. Put sheet in preheated 350° F (175° C) oven and set timer to bake 10 to 12 minutes, or until cookies are just barely golden on the edges.

4. While cookies are baking, sift 1¾ cups (435 ml) confectioners' sugar onto a plate. Place wire rack over piece of wax paper. When cookies are baked, let them cool a few minutes in the pan, then *while they are still warm*, roll them in the sugar on the plate. Set coated cookies on rack over wax paper. When cold, set cookies in a container, sift some more confectioners' sugar over top, and cover with an airtight lid.

MERINGUE ANGEL KISSES

These light cookies are delicate puffs of sweet air. The batter is divided in half, making vanilla kisses (which are slightly chewy inside the crust) and chocolate kisses (which are somewhat drier and crunchier).

GIFT NOTE: Meringue kisses are too fragile to mail. They may be baked ahead and frozen. Packed in an airtight container, kisses stay crisp at least two weeks.

EQUIPMENT:
Measuring cups and spoons
Double boiler
Nut grinder *or* blender
Rubber scraper
2 large mixing bowls
Electric mixer *or* whisk
Large spoon
2 teaspoons
Cookie sheets
Timer
Pancake turner
Wire rack

FOODS YOU WILL NEED:
½ cup semisweet chocolate bits (125 ml; 100 g)
½ cup almonds, blanched and ground (125 ml; 67 g)
3 egg whites
¼ teaspoon salt (1.2 ml)
1 cup granulated sugar (250 ml; 210 g)
¼ teaspoon cream of tartar (1.2 ml)
1 teaspoon vanilla extract (5 ml)
½ teaspoon almond extract (2.5 ml)

Ingredients:

How To:

(To make 48 cookies)

½ cup semisweet chocolate bits (125 ml; 100 g)

½ cup almonds, blanched (125 ml; 67 g)

3 egg whites
¼ teaspoon salt (1.2 ml)
1 cup granulated sugar (250 ml; 210 g)
¼ teaspoon cream of tartar (1.2 ml)

1. Measure chocolate in a double boiler and set on stove over low heat. Melt chocolate, then remove pan from heat and set aside to cool.

2. Grind almonds into a fine powder using a nut grinder *or* a blender. Set nuts aside. Turn oven on to 350° F (175° C).

3. In large mixing bowl, beat egg whites and salt with electric mixer until whites look fluffy. Slowly add sugar a little at a time. Add cream of tartar. Beat

1 teaspoon vanilla extract (5 ml)

½ teaspoon almond extract (2.5 ml)

whites until stiff and satiny. Fold in vanilla extract and all ground almonds. To do this, spoon nuts over whites a little at a time and turn rubber scraper down through mixture to blend. Stir gently to keep as much air as possible in the whites. Spoon half the mixture into the second mixing bowl.

4. Fold melted chocolate into the whites in the second bowl. Gently stir ½ teaspoon (2.5 ml) almond extract into the vanilla-flavored whites in the first bowl.

5. Grease cookie sheets. Make both vanilla and chocolate meringue kisses by scooping up a lump of either flavor batter on one teaspoon. Then use the second teaspoon to push it off onto the greased cookie sheet. Leave some room between cookies, as they spread when baked. Place cookie sheet in preheated 350° F (175° C) oven and set timer to bake 15 minutes. When cookies come out of the oven, remove them from the sheet at once, using a pancake turner. Cool them on a wire rack.

CHOCOLATE NUT DROPS

For chocolate lovers! This delightfully chewy confection is a cross between a cookie and a candy. It contains no flour; the batter is prepared in a pan on the stove, then is baked in the oven.

GIFT NOTE: Packed in plastic bags, these cookies freeze well and so may be made ahead. They are sturdy and will survive mailing. Give Chocolate Nut Drops in a cookie jar with the recipe attached, or on a platter of mixed cookies covered with plastic wrap and tied with a bright ribbon.

EQUIPMENT:
Cookie sheet
Aluminum foil
Wax paper
Measuring cups and spoons
Blender *or* food processor *or* nut grinder
Small bowl
Large saucepan
Wooden spoon
Mixing spoon
Whisk
Rubber scraper
2 teaspoons
Wire rack
Airtight tin *or* cookie jar

FOODS YOU WILL NEED:
1 cup pecan pieces—*or* walnuts *or* hazelnuts (250 ml; 115 g)
1 egg
1 teaspoon vanilla extract *or* almond extract (5 ml)
¼ cup butter (60 g), *plus* extra for greasing baking sheet
¾ cup light brown sugar, packed (185 ml; 168 g)
½ cup semisweet chocolate bits (125 ml; 100 g)

Ingredients:

How To:

(To make about 32 cookies)

1. Turn oven on to 350° F (175° C). Cover cookie sheet with a piece of aluminum foil. Grease foil well with butter. Set aside.

1 cup pecan pieces—*or* walnuts *or* hazelnuts (250 ml; 115 g)

2. Grind nuts finely in blender (a few at a time) *or* in food processor *or* nut grinder. Set nuts aside on wax paper.

1 egg
1 teaspoon vanilla extract *or* almond extract (5 ml)

3. In small bowl, beat together egg and vanilla (*or* almond) extract. Set bowl aside.

¼ cup butter (60 g)

¾ cup light brown sugar (185 ml; 168 g)

½ cup semisweet chocolate bits (125 ml; 100 g)

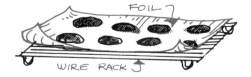

4. In large saucepan, combine butter and sugar. Set on stove over low heat. Stir with wooden spoon until sugar dissolves (about 3 minutes) and mixture comes to a bubbling boil. Turn heat down very low. Add chocolate bits and stir constantly until all melted. Turn off heat. Remove pan from stove. Stir in nuts and beat well.

5. Stir in egg mixture and IMMEDIATELY whisk *or* beat hard about 2 minutes.

6. Drop batter onto greased foil by the teaspoonful. Leave a space as wide as your thumb between cookies as they spread when baking. Place sheet in preheated 350° F (175° C) oven and set timer to bake 8 to 10 minutes. Do not let cookies overbake or bottoms will taste burned.

7. As soon as cookies are done, slide foil off cookie sheet and set it onto wire rack to cool. As soon as cookies are cool, remove them from foil. Cookie tops will be shiny and crackled. Store cold cookies in airtight tin.

NORWEGIAN CASSANDRA COOKIES

Crisp, buttery *Kassandraskaker*, rolled out and cut into shapes, are traditionally made with a crumbly shortbread dough. To make our dough roll and handle more easily, we have added a little milk.

GIFT NOTE: To prepare these cookies ahead, freeze either the un-baked dough or the baked cookies, wrapped airtight. Package baked cookies in an airtight container to retain crispness. *Kassandraskaker* are too easily broken to send through the mail.

EQUIPMENT:
Cookie sheet
Measuring cups and spoons
2 mixing bowls
Small bowl
Electric mixer *or* mixing spoon
Rolling pin
Cookie cutters
Fork
Pastry brush
Spatula
Wire rack

FOODS YOU WILL NEED:
2 eggs
⅔ cup granulated sugar (160 ml; 150 g)
3 tablespoons milk (45 ml)
1 cup (2 sticks) butter (250 ml; 240 g), at room temperature
3 cups all-purpose flour (750 ml; 500 g)

Ingredients:

How To:

(To make 90 cookies)
1 egg
⅔ cup granulated sugar (106 ml; 150 g)
3 tablespoons milk (45 ml)

1 cup (2 sticks) butter (250 ml; 240 g), at room temperature
3 cups all-purpose flour (750 ml; 500 g)

1. Grease cookie sheet with inside of butter wrapper. In large mixing bowl, beat one egg until light. Add sugar and beat well. Then beat in milk.

2. Turn oven on to 350° F (175° C). Wash your hands, as you will be handling the dough. In second bowl, cut butter into small pieces. Add flour. Use your fingers to pinch butter and flour together until they are blended into crumbly bits.

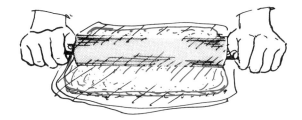

1 egg

3. Add flour mixture to egg-sugar mixture and beat until dough is smooth. If dough feels too sticky to roll out, add a few tablespoons more flour. Or wrap dough and chill in freezer about 30 minutes.

4. Roll out dough about ⅛″ (.25 cm) thick on lightly floured surface. Cut dough with cookie cutters dipped in flour. Set cut cookies on greased sheet.

5. Beat the remaining egg in small bowl. Brush egg over cookies. Then sprinkle cookies with some granulated sugar (or colored sugar crystals). Or bake cookies plain, and decorate with frosting (see page 23 for recipe).

6. Place cookie sheet in preheated 350° F (175° C) oven and set timer to bake 6 to 10 minutes, or until cookies are lightly golden. Lift cookies with spatula and cool them on wire racks. Store them in an airtight container to retain crispness.

COCONUT-HONEY BARS

These moist, chewy bars contain no sugar or shortening; they are sweetened with honey and dried fruit. You can vary the flavor by changing the types of fruits and nuts you use—the recipe is flexible. In the ingredients below, use the orange peel and juice if you like the flavor; or, leave out the orange and you will taste more of the honey.

GIFT NOTE: Coconut-honey bars can be made well ahead of the holidays. Set them on a piece of cardboard to keep them flat, and wrap airtight before freezing them. They also keep well at least a week unfrozen. Package and give the bars in any type of airtight container. Wrapped individually in plastic wrap or foil, the bars can safely be mailed without breaking. (See page 12 for mailing directions.)

EQUIPMENT:

Baking pan 13″ × 9″ × 2″ (34 × 22 × 4.5 cm)
Measuring cups and spoons
Cutting board
Paring knife
Blender or food processor or nut chopper
Wax paper
Grater—optional
2 large mixing bowls
Electric mixer or whisk
Sifter
Mixing spoon
Toothpick or cake tester
Spatula
Airtight container

FOODS YOU WILL NEED:

1 tablespoon margarine (15 ml)
1 cup shelled almonds or walnuts (250 ml; 125 g)
1½ cups shredded coconut, sweetened (3½-ounce can; 99 g)
¾ cup seedless raisins (185 ml; 120 g)
1 cup dried dates, pitted (250 ml; 200 g) or 1 cup dried apricots (250 ml; 150 g)
1 tablespoon orange peel (15 ml)—optional
3 eggs
1 cup honey (250 ml)
1 teaspoon vanilla extract (5 ml)
2 tablespoons orange juice concentrate (30 ml) or 2 teaspoons orange extract (10 ml)—optional
1¼ cups all-purpose flour (310 ml; 205 g)
1 tablespoon dried milk powder (10 ml)
3 tablespoons toasted wheat germ (45 ml)
1 teaspoon baking powder (5 ml)
¼ teaspoon salt (1.2 ml)

Ingredients:

(To make about 40 bars, 1″ × 2″ [2.5 × 5 cm])

1 tablespoon margarine (15 ml)

1 cup shelled almonds *or* walnuts (250 ml; 125 g)

1½ cups shredded coconut, sweetened (3½-ounce can; 99 g)

¾ cup seedless raisins (185 ml; 120 g)

1 cup dried dates, pitted (250 ml; 200 g) *or* 1 cup dried apricots (250 ml; 150 g)

1 tablespoon orange peel (15 ml)—optional

3 eggs

1 cup honey (250 ml)

1 teaspoon vanilla extract (5 ml)

2 tablespoons orange juice concentrate (30 ml) *or* 2 teaspoons orange extract (15 ml)—optional

1¼ cups all-purpose flour (310 ml; 205 g)

1 tablespoon dried milk powder (10 ml)

3 tablespoons toasted wheat germ (45 ml)

1 teaspoon baking powder (5 ml)

¼ teaspoon salt (1.2 ml)

How To:

1. Grease pan with margarine. Turn oven on to 350° F (175° C).

2. In a large bowl, chop the nuts in a nut chopper *or* (working with a few at a time) blender *or* processor. Add nuts to bowl. Measure and add coconut and raisins. Use cutting board and knife to cut up dates *or* apricots into small pieces, then add them to bowl. If you like orange flavor, grate peel of one orange over wax paper, then add to same bowl.

3. In second large mixing bowl, add eggs, honey, vanilla, and if you are using it, orange juice concentrate *or* extract. Beat well with electric mixer *or* whisk.

4. To the egg mixture in the bowl, slowly stir in the flour, dry milk (sifted if lumpy), wheat germ, baking powder, and salt.

5. Stir the fruit-nut mixture into your egg-flour batter and combine well. Then spoon batter into greased pan and spread evenly. Set pan in preheated 350° F (175° C) oven and set timer to bake 30 to 35 minutes, or until lightly golden on top. To test doneness, stick toothpick in center of pan; if toothpick comes out clean, the bars are done.

6. Remove pan from oven and cool on heat-proof surface about 5 minutes. Then cut into 2″ × 1″ bars (2.5 × 5 cm). When thoroughly cold, lift bars from pan with spatula and store them in airtight container, or wrap them airtight and freeze. To serve, bars may be left plain or topped with a light sifting of powdered sugar.

SNICKERDOODLES

These old-fashioned American butter cookies, sometimes also known as Snipperdoodles, are cinnamon-coated. As a variation, they can be made with nuts or raisins.

GIFT NOTE: Pack Snickerdoodles in a cookie jar or covered tin with the recipe attached. Snickerdoodles freeze well and may be made ahead.

EQUIPMENT:
Cookie sheet
Measuring cups and spoons
Small bowl
Mixing bowl
Rubber scraper
Electric mixer *or* mixing spoon
Rolling pin
2 teaspoons
Wax paper
Pancake turner
Wire rack
Airtight tin

FOODS YOU WILL NEED:
1 cup butter (250 ml; 240 g), at room temperature, *plus* extra for greasing cookie sheet
1½ cups granulated sugar (375 ml; 315 g)
2 eggs
¼ cup milk (60 ml)
1 teaspoon vanilla extract (5 ml)
3 cups all-purpose flour (750 ml; 500 g)
½ teaspoon salt (2.5 ml)
¾ teaspoon baking soda (3.7 ml)
1 teaspoon cream of tartar (5 ml)
Topping:
3 tablespoons (45 ml) *each:*
granulated sugar and cinnamon

Ingredients:

(To make 100 cookies)

1 cup (2 sticks) butter (250 ml; 240 g), at room temperature

1½ cups granulated sugar (375 ml; 315 g)

2 eggs

¼ cup milk (60 ml)

1 teaspoon vanilla extract (5 ml)

3 cups all-purpose flour (750 ml; 500 g)

½ teaspoon salt (2.5 ml)

¾ teaspoon baking soda (3.7 ml)

1 teaspoon cream of tartar (5 ml)

3 tablespoons (45 ml) *each*: cinnamon and sugar

NOTE: If dough feels too soft to roll, chill it in refrigerator 30 minutes.

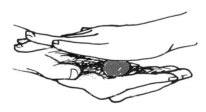

VARIATION: IN STEP 3 YOU CAN ADD 1 TEASPOON NUTMEG PLUS 1 CUP CHOPPED NUTS OR RAISINS

How To:

1. Turn oven on to 375° F (190° C). Grease cookie sheet and set it aside.

2. In mixing bowl, beat together butter and sugar until creamy. Add eggs, milk, and vanilla and beat until smooth.

3. Slowly stir in flour, salt, baking soda, and cream of tartar. Beat until well blended and dough forms a ball. Wash your hands, as you will be touching dough.

4. In a small bowl, combine sugar and cinnamon to make topping. Set aside.

5. Use your hands to pick up small lumps of dough and roll them into balls. Roll balls in cinnamon-sugar topping, then place them on greased cookie sheet.

6. Place cookie sheet in preheated 375° F (190° C) oven and set timer to bake 8 to 10 minutes. While still warm, lift cookies from sheet with pancake turner and cool them on wire rack. Store in airtight container.

Candies

APRICOT-COCONUT SNOWBALLS

No baking needed for these delicious and highly nutritious candies—just combine ingredients and roll into balls.

GIFT NOTE: These snowballs keep well and can be made a week or so ahead of the holidays. Pack in a transparent covered jar and store in a cool dry place.

EQUIPMENT:
Measuring cups and spoons
Large mixing bowl
Small bowl
Blender *or* food processor
Rubber scraper
Spoon
Wax paper
Tray
Covered jar

FOODS YOU WILL NEED:
1 cup shredded coconut, sweetened (250 ml; 120 g)
2 cups dried apricots (11-ounce box; 311 g)
4 teaspoons lemon juice (20 ml)
4 tablespoons toasted wheat germ (60 ml)
4 tablespoons dry milk (60 ml)
4 tablespoons honey (60 ml)

Ingredients:

How To:

(To make 40 balls)

1 cup shredded coconut, sweetened (250 ml; 120 g)

2 cups dried apricots (11-ounce box; 311 g)

4 teaspoons lemon juice (20 ml)

4 tablespoons toasted wheat germ (60 ml)

4 tablespoons dry milk (60 ml)

4 tablespoons honey (60 ml)

1. Measure ¾ cup (185 ml) coconut into large mixing bowl and put the rest into the small bowl.

2. Using the blender *or* food processor, grind the apricots—½ cup (125 ml) at a time—into small pieces. Place ground apricots into large bowl with coconut.

Finally, roll balls in small bowl of coconut. Let balls stand to air-dry several hours, until firm.

3. Add lemon juice, wheat germ, dry milk, and honey to apricot-coconut mixture in large bowl. Mix well. Dampen your hands and roll mixture into small balls. Set balls on a wax-paper-covered tray.

BUTTER MINTS

No cooking is needed for this fun-to-make candy. Even the youngest cook can help hand-shape the mints, which dry in the air.

GIFT NOTE: After mints are air-dried, they remain fresh up to a month in a covered tin. Variation: Shape colored mints into small egg shapes, or model them into fruit forms like marzipan.

EQUIPMENT:
Measuring cups and spoons
Mixing bowl
Electric mixer *or* mixing spoon
Sifter
Wax paper
Table fork
Cookie sheet *or* tray

FOODS YOU WILL NEED:
⅓ cup light corn syrup (80 ml)
¼ cup (½ stick) butter (60 ml; 60 g), at room temperature
1 teaspoon peppermint extract (5 ml)
½ teaspoon salt (2.5 ml)
1 pound confectioners' sugar (4¾ cups; 785 g)
Food coloring

Ingredients:

(To make about 70 mints)

⅓ cup light corn syrup (80 ml)
¼ cup (½ stick) butter (60 ml; 60 g), at room temperature
1 teaspoon peppermint extract (5 ml)
½ teaspoon salt (2.5 ml)
1 pound confectioners' sugar (4¾ cups; 785 g)

Food coloring: red (or substitute beet *or* raspberry *or* cranberry juice); green; yellow (or substitute frozen orange juice concentrate, undiluted)

2. On wax paper, divide dough into four equal parts. Leave one part white; add one drop of food coloring or a substitute to the other parts. Knead each color into the dough until it is an even tone throughout.

How To:

1. Wash hands, as you will be handling dough. In mixing bowl, combine corn syrup, butter, peppermint extract, and salt. Mix well. Sift in sugar and stir slowly to combine. Mix dough together with your hands until a smooth ball can be formed. If your hands get sticky, coat them lightly with confectioners' sugar.

3. Shape the dough into small balls. Set the balls on a wax-paper-covered cookie sheet or tray. Flatten balls by pressing with tines of a fork. Let mints sit out in the air overnight or at least 4 hours to air-dry.

MARZIPAN

This Marzipan candy is quick and easy to make and requires no cooking.

GIFT NOTE: Marzipan keeps well several weeks stored in an airtight container. For a unique gift, fill a homemade chocolate box (see page 48) with marzipan candies.

EQUIPMENT:
Can opener
Large mixing bowl
Measuring cups and spoons
Sifter
Toothpick
Wax paper
Clean new paintbrush (small size)

FOODS YOU WILL NEED:
8-ounce can pure almond paste (1 cup; 220 g)
1 egg white
2 teaspoons almond extract (10 ml)
2 to 2½ cups confectioners' sugar (625 ml; 315 g), sifted
Whole cloves
Food coloring
Water

Ingredients:

(To make about 2 cups marzipan [500 ml] for about 40 candies)

8-ounce can pure almond paste (1 cup; 220 g)
1 egg white
2 teaspoons almond extract (10 ml)
2 cups confectioners' sugar, sifted (500 ml; 200 g)

2. On sugared counter, knead dough until smooth and satiny by folding it and pushing it away from you with the heels of your hands.

3. Break off small lumps of dough and mold like clay, shaping into balls *or* bananas, pears, strawberries, peaches *or* animals. Use toothpick to help mold. Set shapes on

How To:

1. Wash your hands, as you will be touching dough. Open can and crumble almond paste into bowl. Add egg white, almond extract, and 2 cups (500 ml; 200g) confectioners' sugar, sifted in. Mix dough together with spoon *or* sugared hands until it forms a ball. Sift in extra sugar if dough needs to be drier.

wax paper. Poke whole cloves into fruits for stems. To color shapes, brush on food coloring thinned with water. Let marzipan stand to air-dry several hours or overnight. Store airtight.

CHRISTMAS TREES

Even the youngest holiday cooks will enjoy hand-shaping these marshmallow and cereal trees. Stand them in a row on gold doilies with red candy trim and a dusting of sugar "snow" to make a party centerpiece.

GIFT NOTE: Gift-pack trees in plastic wrap set in a protective box. Smaller stand-up figures can be made by pressing cereal mixture into cookie cutters.

EQUIPMENT:
Measuring cups and spoons
Double boiler
Long-handled wooden spoon
Large mixing bowl
Rubber scraper
Paper or foil doilies—optional
Cookie cutters—optional
Sifter

FOODS YOU WILL NEED:
¼ cup (½ stick) margarine (60 ml; 60 g)
40 regular-sized marshmallows
6 to 7 ounces cereal (5 to 6 cups, 600 g), such as Rice Krispies or Puffed Rice or Puffed Millet
½ cup toasted wheat germ (125 ml)
⅓ cup tiny cinnamon hot candies (80 ml)
Confectioners' sugar

Ingredients:

(To make 8 trees 5" tall [13 cm] or about 12 cookie cutter shapes)

¼ cup (½ stick) margarine (60 ml; 60 g)

40 regular-sized marshmallows

6 to 7 ounces cereal (5 to 6 cups, 600 g), such as Rice Krispies *or* Puffed Rice *or* Puffed Millet

½ cup toasted wheat germ (125 ml)

¼ cup tiny cinnamon hot candies (60 ml). Save extra cinnamon hots for trimming trees.

How To:

1. In double boiler, combine and melt margarine and marshmallows stirring occasionally with wooden spoon over medium heat. Mixture will be completely melted in 10 to 15 minutes. Once melted, stir and cook about 2 minutes longer.

2. While marshmallows are melting, combine cereal, wheat germ, and most of the cinnamon hots in large mixing bowl.

3. When marshmallow mixture is ready, remove pan from stove. Use rubber scraper to scoop melted mixture into bowl. Stir everything together well with wooden spoon. Stir until mixture develops spiderweb-like threads between cereal bits.

4. Grease your hands with a little margarine. Break off a lump of cereal mixture and roll it into a ball about as wide as the palm of your hand. Then roll the top into a point to make a cone-shaped tree. Set tree on doily and top with one cinnamon hot pressed into tree tip. Sift a tiny bit of confectioners' sugar over tree top for "snow." Repeat to make more trees; or press mixture into greased cookie cutters. Fill to top of cutter, press firmly, then press shape out of cutter.

CONE

SUGAR SNOW

COOKIE CUTTER SHAPES:

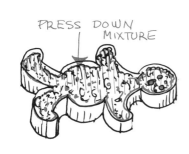

PRESS DOWN MIXTURE

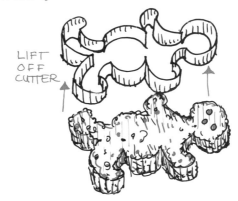

LIFT OFF CUTTER

STAND UP SHAPE

PEANUT BRITTLE

The crunchy confection everyone loves is surprisingly easy to make.

GIFT NOTE: Peanut brittle stays crisp and fresh a month or longer when packed airtight in a decorative tin or jar. If mailed, it will crack easily unless packed tightly—cushion with plastic bags of popcorn.

EQUIPMENT:
Measuring cups and spoons
Jelly roll pan *or* cookie sheet
Spatula
2 long-handled wooden spoons
Large saucepan with lid
Table knife
Wax paper
Candy thermometer *or* glass of ice water
Paper towels
Airtight container

FOODS YOU WILL NEED:
Vegetable oil (to grease utensils)
1 cup granulated sugar (250 ml; 210 g)
½ cup water (125 ml)
½ cup light corn syrup (125 ml)
1 cup peanuts, salted and dry roasted (250 ml; 140 g)
1½ tablespoons butter (22 ml)

Ingredients:

(To make about 1 pound candy [410 g])

Vegetable oil

1 cup granulated sugar (250 ml; 210 g)
½ cup water (125 ml)
½ cup light corn syrup (125 ml)
1 cup peanuts, salted and dry roasted (250 ml; 140 g)

How To:

1. Spread a coating of oil on jelly roll pan *or* cookie sheet, as well as on spatula, and one wooden spoon. Set them aside.

2. Add sugar, water, and corn syrup to large saucepan. Cover. Set pan on stove over high heat and bring to a boil (about 2 to 3 minutes). Then uncover, lower heat slightly, and stir with second wooden spoon (not oiled) until all sugar is dissolved. Stir in peanuts.

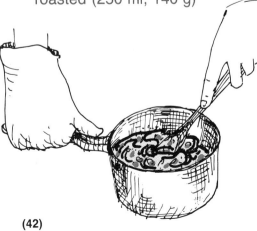

1½ tablespoons butter (22 ml),
cut in pieces

3. Leave cover off pan. Turn heat to medium-high and boil syrup until it turns a golden color (about 8 to 10 minutes) and thermometer reads 295° F (146° C), or until a drop of syrup spooned into ice water forms a hard ball that *cracks* when broken.

4. When syrup has reached the "hard-crack stage" described above, remove pan from stove and set on heat-proof surface. Add cut-up butter and stir until entirely melted.

5. Pour syrup onto oiled pan and *immediately* use oiled spoon and spatula to pat and spread mixture into a very thin layer covering the pan. As soon as the candy becomes hard and crisp (about 5 minutes at room temperature on a cool, dry day; refrigerate in summer), use oiled spatula to pry it up from pan. Break candy into large sections and wipe them gently with paper towels to blot off the excess oil. Then break candy into bite-sized pieces and store in airtight container.

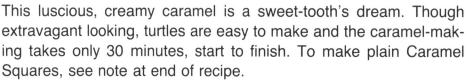

CARAMEL-PECAN TURTLES *or* CARAMEL SQUARES

This luscious, creamy caramel is a sweet-tooth's dream. Though extravagant looking, turtles are easy to make and the caramel-making takes only 30 minutes, start to finish. To make plain Caramel Squares, see note at end of recipe.

GIFT NOTE: Turtles should be stored in single layers between sheets of wax paper or plastic wrap, in decorative tins or boxes. Keep in cool, dry place.

EQUIPMENT:
Measuring cups and spoons
3-quart saucepan
Candy thermometer *or* glass of ice water
Wooden spoon
Jelly roll pan *or* cookie sheet *or* marble slab
2 teaspoons
Small saucepan *or* double boiler
Plastic wrap *or* wax paper

FOODS YOU WILL NEED:
1½ cups heavy cream (375 ml)
½ cup granulated sugar (125 ml; 105 g)
½ cup light brown sugar, packed (125 ml; 112 g)
¾ cup light corn syrup (185 ml)
Pinch of salt
½ teaspoon vanilla extract (2.5 ml)
2 tablespoons butter (30 ml) *plus* butter to grease pans *or* slab
3 cups pecan halves (750 ml; 345 g)
1 small package semisweet chocolate bits (6 ounces; 250 ml; 175 g)

Ingredients:

How To:

(To make about 36 turtles)

¾ cup heavy cream (185 ml)
½ cup granulated sugar (125 ml; 105 g)
½ cup light brown sugar (125 ml; 112 g), packed
¾ cup light corn syrup (185 ml)
Pinch of salt

1. To make caramel, in large saucepan combine ¾ cup (185 ml) cream, white and brown sugar, corn syrup, and salt. Set pan on stove over medium heat and stir mixture with wooden spoon until sugar is dissolved.

2. If you have a candy thermometer, set it in pan now. Or place a glass of water with ice cubes alongside stove. Cook syrup over medium-high heat about 10 minutes,

stirring occasionally, until thermometer reads 234° F (114° C), or until a soft ball is formed when a drop of syrup is spooned into ice water.

¾ cup heavy cream (185 ml)
½ teaspoon vanilla extract (2.5 ml)
2 tablespoons butter (30 ml)
3 cups pecan halves (750 ml; 345 g)
1 small package semisweet chocolate bits (6 ounces; 250 ml; 175 g)

3. Keeping pan on stove boiling slowly, stir in remaining ¾ cup (185 ml) cream. Cook and stir about 5 more minutes on high heat, until thermometer reads 244° F (118° C), or until a hard ball is formed when a drop of syrup is spooned into ice water.

4. Remove pan from stove and set on heat-proof surface. Stir in vanilla and butter; stir until butter melts.
    Grease jelly roll pan or cookie sheet or marble slab with extra butter.

5. For each turtle, arrange four pecan halves, as shown, on greased surface. Split one nut in half lengthwise and set one sliver at the top for turtle's head, one at bottom for tail. Drip a spoonful of hot caramel over center of nuts. Tips of nut feet, head, and tail should poke out of caramel. Let turtles sit untouched until caramel firms up.

6. While turtles set, place chocolate bits in small saucepan (or in double boiler) on stove over low heat. Melt chocolate. Then spoon a little melted chocolate over the back of each turtle. Let stand until chocolate is hard. Wrap in plastic or wax paper. Store.
    NOTE: Caramel Squares: Instead of pecan turtles, 1½ pounds (675 g) of plain caramel candies can be made from this recipe. In step 4, pour hot caramel into a greased 8″ (20 cm) square pan, cool 30 minutes, and cut into small squares with a knife dipped in water. Set pan in refrigerator until caramel is firm, then break pieces apart where cut and wrap in plastic wrap.

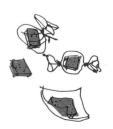

PRALINES

Pecan pralines, a New Orleans specialty, are a rich and very sweet candy.

GIFT NOTE: Pack pralines in flat layers in an airtight container. Store in a cool, dry place. Pralines are fragile, so wrap them individually in wax paper and cushion them well if you plan to mail them (see page 12 for mailing directions). NOTE: To make praline powder for an ice-cream topping (or soufflé flavoring), grind several pralines in the blender *or* food processor. Pack powder in a decorative glass bottle. Label: "Praline Powder–dessert topping."

EQUIPMENT:
2 large flat platters *or* a marble slab
Wax paper
Large saucepan
Measuring cups and spoons
Wooden spoon
Candy thermometer *or* glass of ice water
Mixing spoon
Airtight container

FOODS YOU WILL NEED:
2 cups light brown sugar (500 ml; 450 g)
¼ cup water (60 ml)
¼ cup butter (60 g) *plus* extra to butter platters
2 cups pecans, broken into small pieces (500 ml; 230 g)

Ingredients:

How To:

(To make about 1 pound [440 g] pralines)

2 cups light brown sugar (500 ml; 450 g)
¼ cup water (60 ml)
¼ cup butter (60 g)

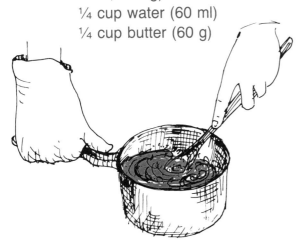

1. Heavily butter 2 platters *or* marble slab *or* 2 large sheets wax paper set on a table. Set them aside.

2. In large saucepan, measure sugar, water, and butter. Stir with wooden spoon over low heat until sugar is dissolved and mixture comes to a boil.

2 cups pecans, broken into small pieces (500 ml; 230 g)

3. Stir in nuts. Place candy thermometer in pan, tilted so tip does not rest on pan bottom, *or* set glass of ice water beside stove. Turn heat to medium. Boil syrup slowly about 5 minutes, stirring occasionally with wooden spoon, until temperature reaches 234° F (114° C), or until a drop of syrup spooned into ice water forms a soft ball. Remove pan from stove and set on heat-proof surface.

4. Immediately, form pralines by dropping one tablespoon of syrup at a time onto greased surface. Candies can be large or bite-sized, as you like. NOTE: If mixture gets hard and crystalizes before you are through shaping candies, add in a few drops of hot water and stir well. Let pralines set until cold and hard before packing.

CHOCOLATE BOX

This is the ultimate Gift to Eat: a chocolate gift box! Fill it with home-made candies for the favorite person on your gift list.

GIFT NOTE: Chocolate boxes can be made ahead and, set in a protective carton, frozen. They are delicate, but not as fragile as you might think. To give as a gift, set chocolate box inside a cardboard box, cushioned by tissue *or* plastic wrap.

EQUIPMENT:
Measuring cups and spoons
Double boiler
Soup bowl (6″ diameter [15 cm])
Ruler and tape measure
Pencil
Scissors
Tape
Wax paper

2 large cookie sheets (14″ × 17″ [35.5 × 43 cm])
Rubber scraper
Spatula
Paring knife
Spoon
Toothpick

FOODS YOU WILL NEED:
12 ounces semisweet chocolate *or* 12 squares Baker's chocolate (480 g)

How to:

---

1. Melt chocolate in double boiler. While melting, prepare box patterns.

2. To make pattern for box top, set soup bowl upside down on sheet of wax paper and draw a pencil line around edge, as shown. Repeat on a second piece of paper for box bottom.

   For box sides, cut one wax-paper strip 4″ × 24″ (10 × 61 cm). Inside this shape, draw a strip 2″ wide and 20″ long (5 × 51 cm). Also cut a test strip of paper about 2″ × 4″ (5 × 10 cm).

(To make one 6″ [15 cm] round box)

BOX TOP AND BOX BOTTOM PATTERNS

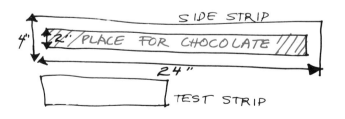

SIDE STRIP

4″   2″ PLACE FOR CHOCOLATE

24″

TEST STRIP

3. Make a paper cone for decorating box. Cut a piece of wax paper 6″ × 9″ (15 × 22.5 cm). Roll paper into a cone with the tip at the center of one long edge as shown. Tape cone to hold it together. Cut a *tiny* piece off tip to make opening hole. This cone can also be used as a frosting tube.

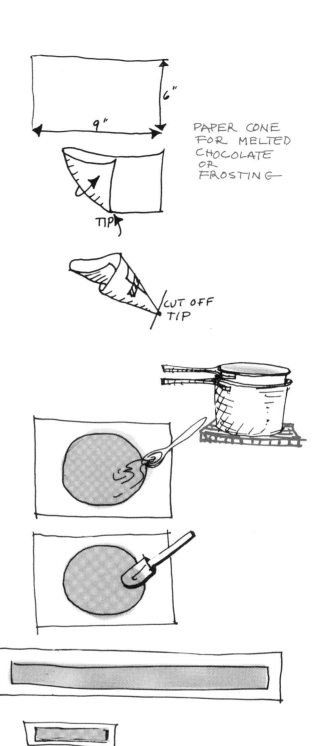

PAPER CONE FOR MELTED CHOCOLATE OR FROSTING

TIP

CUT OFF TIP

4. When chocolate is melted, turn off stove. Set pan of chocolate on heat-proof surface.

Put all paper patterns pencil-side down so you can see lines but chocolate won't touch them. Long side strip should be placed on diagonal to fit on cookie sheet. Use spoon to dribble melted chocolate over marked lines. Then fill inner areas and spread chocolate smooth (about ⅛″ [.25 cm] thick) with rubber scraper *or* spatula. Also spread chocolate on test strip.

5. Place sheets with chocolate in refrigerator. Set a timer to check chocolate in 10 to 15 minutes. Chocolate is

NOTE: It doesn't matter if chocolate goes outside the pattern lines, as the shapes will be trimmed neatly later.

ready to use when set (hard) *but still flexible*; it will have lost its shine. Try touching and bending test-strip chocolate.

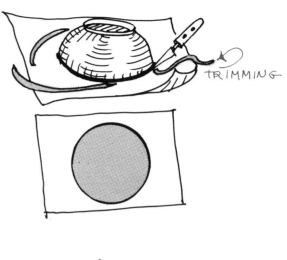

TRIMMING

6. When ready, remove chocolate from refrigerator. Place soup bowl upside down over one chocolate disk and cut around its edge with the tip of a paring knife to trim shape. Peel away trimming. Repeat with second disk. To trim box sides, place ruler flat on top of long chocolate strip. Move ruler along as you cut against its straight edge trimming strip neatly, 2" (5 cm) wide, 20" (51 cm) long.

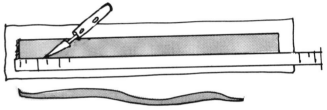

7. To assemble box: Set one disk flat. Lift long strip (paper on outside) and bend it around the edge of the disk (up against it, not on top of it). Peel off paper. Gently mold strip of chocolate to base of disk. NOTE: If strip does not bend easily, it is either too cold or too thick. Warm it up by placing it on cookie sheet in preheated 350° F (175° C) oven for *one minute*. Ends of strip should meet; if they overlap, trim with hot knife. Seal ends together with melted chocolate.

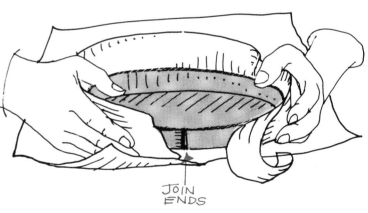

JOIN ENDS

NOTE: Patch any broken chocolate pieces by spreading with melted chocolate.

8. Spoon several tablespoons of melted chocolate into paper cone. Roll down opened end to close. Squeeze cone gently, forcing out a line of chocolate inside box at edge where disk meets side. Then lightly smooth this line with the tip of your finger, joining side and bottom of box. Let chocolate set without moving box.

9. To decorate box top, set second disk flat. Draw a simple scroll or flower design on top with toothpick. Add melted chocolate to cone if necessary and squeeze out chocolate lines over drawn lines. Let chocolate set without moving.

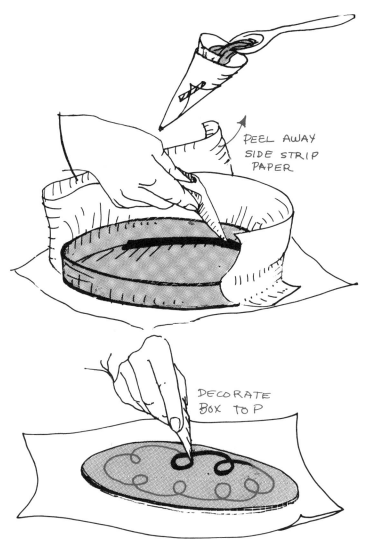

PEEL AWAY SIDE STRIP PAPER

DECORATE BOX TOP

GENERAL CHOCOLATE NOTES:

● Once melted, chocolate will stay soft in the pot, at room temperature, about 40 minutes. If chocolate hardens, return to heat and remelt.

● Remember, you can patch broken pieces of chocolate by spreading with melted chocolate "glue."

● Do not drip any water on chocolate box or it will leave light-colored spots. Blot water spots with tissue immediately.

● Leftover trimmings and scraps of chocolate can be melted in double boiler, poured into muffin cups, and refrigerated until hard. Use for baking.

Cakes and Breads

APPLESAUCE-NUT CAKE

This is a moist, spicy cake chock full of crunchy fruit and nuts.

GIFT NOTE: One recipe will make as many as five small gift loaves trimmed with sugar glaze and candied fruit. Bake ahead of time and freeze cakes in plastic bags. For a gift, wrap with a loaf pan and a recipe.

EQUIPMENT:

Either 5 baby loaf pans (6″ × 3½″ × 2″ [15 × 9 × 5 cm]) *or* one regular loaf (9″ × 5″ x 3″ [23 × 12.5 × 7.5 cm]) plus 2 baby loaves

Measuring cups and spoons

Small, medium, and large mixing bowls

Sifter

Slotted spoon *or* electric mixer

Large spoon

Rubber scraper

Timer

Cake tester *or* toothpick

Potholders

Table knife

Wire rack

FOODS YOU WILL NEED:

½ cup (1 stick) butter *or* margarine (125 ml; 120 g) at room temperature, *plus* extra for greasing pans

2½ cups all-purpose flour (625 ml; 405 g), *plus* extra for coating pans

1 teaspoon baking powder (5 ml)

1½ teaspoons baking soda (7.5 ml)

1½ teaspoons salt (7.5 ml)

1 cup light brown sugar (250 ml; 225 g)

1 cup granulated white sugar (250 ml; 210 g)

2 eggs

1 cup applesauce (250 ml)

¼ cup wheat germ (60 ml)

¼ cup plain yogurt (60 ml)

½ cup apple juice or cider (125 ml)

Spices:

½ teaspoon (2.5 ml) *each*: nutmeg, cinnamon, ground cardamom

¼ teaspoon ground cloves (1.2 ml)

½ cup (125 ml) *each*: seedless raisins (80 g), chopped nuts (65 g), and chopped dates *or* dried figs (100 g)

Ingredients:

(To make 1 regular and 2 baby loaves, or *5 baby loaves)*

2½ cups all-purpose flour (625 ml; 405 g)
1 teaspoon baking powder (5 ml)
1½ teaspoons baking soda (7.5 ml)
1½ teaspoons salt (7.5 ml)

½ cup (1 stick) butter *or* margarine (125 ml; 120 g), at room temperature
1 cup light brown sugar, packed (250 ml; 225 g)
1 cup granulated white sugar (250 ml; 210 g)

2 eggs
1 cup applesauce (250 ml)
¼ cup wheat germ (60 ml)
¼ cup plain yogurt (60 ml)
½ cup apple juice *or* cider (125 ml)
Spices:
½ teaspoon (2.5 ml) *each:* nutmeg, cinnamon, ground cardamom
¼ teaspoon ground cloves (1.2 ml)

How To:

1. Turn oven on to 350° F (175° C). Generously grease baking pans with butter *or* margarine. Then sprinkle insides of pans with some flour. Tip pans until flour coats grease, then turn pans upside down and shake out extra flour. Set pans aside.

2. Sift flour, baking powder, soda, and salt into medium-sized bowl. Set it aside.

3. In large bowl, beat together butter *or* margarine and sugar using slotted spoon *or* electric mixer on medium speed. Beat until smooth.

4. Break eggs into a measuring cup, then add them to butter-sugar mixture and beat well. Add applesauce, wheat germ, yogurt, juice, and spices. Beat until well blended.

½ cup (125 ml) *each*: seedless raisins (80 g), chopped nuts (65 g), and chopped dates *or* dried figs (100 g) NOTE: You can also use a combination of dried dates, figs, and apricots.

2 BABY LOAVES

ONE REGULAR LOAF

5. In small bowl, combine raisins, nuts, and dried fruits. Sprinkle on about 3 tablespoons of flour mixture and stir to coat and separate all pieces. This will keep them from sinking when baked.

6. Spoon flour mixture a little at a time into egg-applesauce mixture. Beat slowly after each addition of flour. When batter is thoroughly blended, stir in nut-fruit mixture.

7. Spoon batter into prepared pans, filling two-thirds full. Place pans in preheated 350°F (175° C) oven and set timer to bake baby loaves 45 minutes, regular loaf about 60 minutes. To test doneness, poke testing stick in cake center; if it comes out dry, cake is done. If doughy, bake another 5 to 10 minutes and retest.

8. Use potholders to remove cakes from oven. Cool cakes about 5 minutes, then run a table knife blade around edge of each cake to separate it from its pan. Tip cake out of pan and cool, right side up, on wire rack. When cold, frost with Orange Sugar Glaze (see page 73 for recipe). Press halved cherries and almonds into glaze for trim. Wrap and give (or freeze) after glaze hardens. NOTE: This cake cuts most easily the day after baking.

ORANGE SUGAR GLAZE

BÛCHE DE NOËL

In France, this cake, or Yule Log, is a traditional part of the Christmas celebration. It is very realistic looking: the yellow cake is rolled with dark butter cream filling, frosted and coated with rough chocolate bark, and trimmed with marzipan mushrooms and leaves. Both the bark and the marzipan can be made ahead and frozen, but the Yule Log is best made and served fresh. If necessary, the Yule Log can be completely made ahead, wrapped in foil, and frozen up to two weeks. This is a good project for several cooks to work on together, for it is time-consuming but well worth the effort.

GIFT NOTE: Make the Yule Log as the dessert centerpiece for your Christmas party, or pack it carefully in a cake-carrier and bring it as a gift for a friend's party.

EQUIPMENT:
Wax paper
Scissors
Jelly roll pan
Clean linen dishtowel
Large mixing bowl
Electric mixer or eggbeater
Measuring cups and spoons
Sifter
Mixing spoon
Rubber scraper
Timer
Cake tester or toothpick
Potholders
Table knife and knife with serrated blade
Double boiler
Large spoon and teaspoon
Table fork
Vegetable peeler
Platter
Plastic wrap

FOODS YOU WILL NEED:

For Cake:
Butter or margarine for greasing pan
⅓ cup confectioners' sugar (80 ml; 40g)
4 large eggs
¾ cup granulated sugar (185 ml; 165 g)
1 teaspoon vanilla extract (5 ml)
¾ cup all-purpose flour (185 ml; 120 g)
1 teaspoon baking powder (5 ml)
¼ teaspoon salt (1.2 ml)

For Mocha Butter Cream Frosting:
3 ounces (3 squares) unsweetened *or* semisweet Baker's chocolate (75 g)
2 teaspoons vanilla extract (10 ml)
1½ teaspoons instant coffee (7.5 ml)
¾ cup butter, at room temperature (180 g)
3 cups confectioners' sugar, sifted (750 ml; 300 g)
3–6 tablespoons heavy cream or milk (45–90 ml)

For Chocolate Bark and Mushrooms:
Thick bar of semisweet milk chocolate candy *or* 3 ounces semisweet Baker's chocolate (75 g)
Marzipan (see recipe on page 39)

Ingredients:	How To:

(To make one 10″ [25.5 cm] long rolled cake; serves 8–10)

⅓ cup confectioners' sugar (80 ml; 40 g)

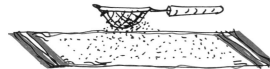

4 large eggs

¾ cup granulated sugar (185 ml; 165 g)
1 teaspoon vanilla extract (5 ml)

¾ cup all-purpose flour (185 ml; 120 g)
1 teaspoon baking powder (5 ml)
¼ teaspoon salt (1.2 ml)

How To:

1. Turn oven on to 375°F (190°C). Cut a sheet of wax paper the same size as the jelly roll pan. Grease the inside of the pan generously with butter or margarine. Then set the paper on the greased surface and grease the top of the paper. Set prepared pan aside.

2. Set out a clean linen dishtowel on your work table. Sift over it an even layer of confectioners' sugar.

3. Break eggs, one at a time, into mixing bowl and beat with electric mixer or eggbeater until very light and foamy. Beat a full 3 minutes.

4. Add sugar and beat a full 2 minutes more until thick and pale yellow. Stir in vanilla.

5. Sift together flour, baking powder, and salt on a piece of wax paper. Spoon this mixture, a little at a time, into egg-sugar mixture.

6. Fold in the flour by turning the spoon upside down as you pull it slowly through the mixture. You want to keep the air bubbles in the batter. Then spread batter onto prepared pan, smoothing it well into the pan corners.

7. Place pan in center of 375°F (190°C) oven and set timer to bake 12–13 minutes, or until cake shrinks away from pan sides slightly. When done, a cake tester stuck into cake center should come out clean.

8. Remove cake from oven with potholders. Immediately, run a table knife blade around inside edge of pan to loosen cake. Then turn pan upside down on top of sugared dishtowel. Lift up pan. Cake will remain on towel. Immediately peel wax paper off cake. Discard paper.

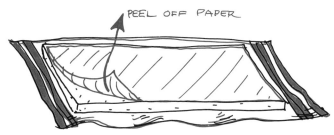

PEEL OFF PAPER

9. Use knife with serrated blade to trim away stiff outer edge—about ¼" (.5 cm) thick—all around cake. You can surely think of something to do with the cut pieces!

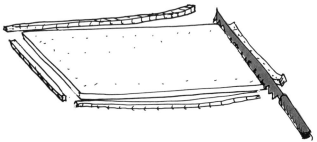

10. Pick up the towel at one side of the cake and roll them together as shown. The towel is rolled inside the cake. Place roll seam down to cool while you prepare the frosting, chocolate bark, and marzipan.

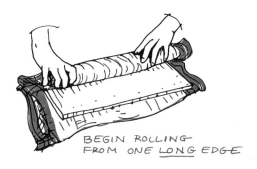

BEGIN ROLLING FROM ONE LONG EDGE

MOCHA BUTTER CREAM FROSTING

Ingredients:

3 ounces (3 squares) unsweetened *or* semisweet Baker's chocolate (75 g)

2 teaspoons vanilla extract (10 ml)

1½ teaspoons instant coffee (7.5 ml)

¾ cup butter, at room temperature (180 g)

3 cups confectioners' sugar, sifted (750 ml; 300 g)

3–6 tablespoons heavy cream *or* milk (45–90 ml)

How To:

1. Set chocolate in double boiler over medium heat until chocolate melts. Then remove section with chocolate from double boiler and set it aside to cool slightly.

2. Add both vanilla and coffee to a cup and stir until coffee dissolves. Set cup aside.

3. In a large bowl, use electric mixer to beat butter until soft and creamy. Add chocolate with a rubber scraper, then add vanilla-coffee mixture. Beat together about 3 minutes, until very smooth and creamy.

4. Add sifted sugar, one cup at a time, to chocolate mixture in bowl. Beat slowly between each addition. Finally, add cream or milk, one tablespoon at a time, until frosting reaches a smooth, spreading consistency. If it gets stiff later, beat in a little more liquid. Cover frosting with plastic wrap so it will stay soft while you prepare trimming. If it must wait a long time, refrigerate it, then bring to room temperature and beat to soften before spreading on cake.

CHOCOLATE BARK

Chocolate bark is made with slivers and curls of dark chocolate which are stuck into the frosted cake. Here are two methods for making bark; try whichever seems easier to you.

Method 1

Have a thick chocolate candy bar at room temperature. Pull a vegetable peeler across the flat top or the side edge of the chocolate, shaving off curls. Press fairly hard as you pull the peeler through the chocolate. If the chocolate is too hard and cold to peel properly, warm the bar between the palms of your hands or set it in a warm oven for a minute. Place curls on plate and refrigerate them until needed.

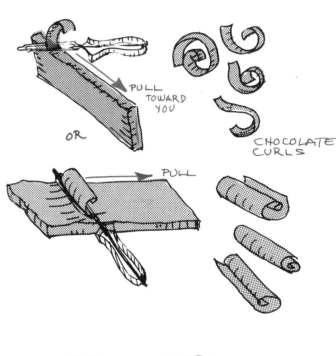

Method 2

1. Melt 3 squares Baker's chocolate (75 g) in double boiler. Spread melted chocolate into a thin layer on a piece of wax paper.

2. Set paper on a plate in the refrigerator or freezer about 4–5 minutes, or until chocolate is very hard.

3. When chocolate is hard, hold the paper in your hands and bend it back and forth over a platter or tray. Chocolate will crack into long slivers and pop off the paper. Refrigerate until needed.

MARZIPAN MUSHROOMS AND LEAVES

If you want to add this traditional French touch, follow the recipe for marzipan on page 39. Leave marzipan white for mushrooms, and tint a part green for leaves.

Mushrooms should be roughly 1″ to 2″ (2.5–5 cm) tall when completed, and are made by combining a fat, rolled stem with a cup-shaped cap. Fasten the pieces by moistening touch-points with a drop of water, then pressing together. Shape leaves with your hands or cut them with a knife from flattened dough.

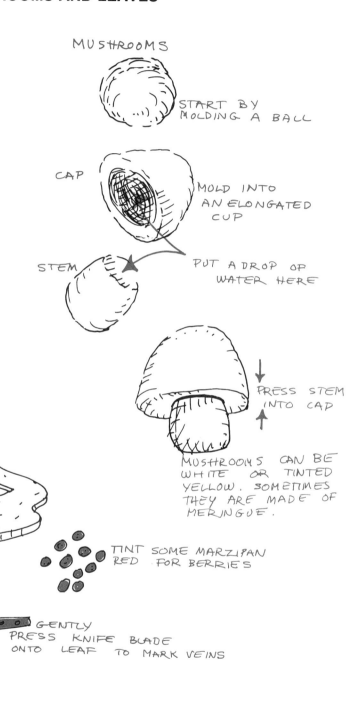

MUSHROOMS

START BY MOLDING A BALL

CAP

MOLD INTO AN ELONGATED CUP

STEM

PUT A DROP OF WATER HERE

PRESS STEM INTO CAP

MUSHROOMS CAN BE WHITE OR TINTED YELLOW. SOMETIMES THEY ARE MADE OF MERINGUE.

TINT SOME MARZIPAN RED FOR BERRIES

LEAVES

HOLLY LEAVES

GENTLY PRESS KNIFE BLADE ONTO LEAF TO MARK VEINS

TO ASSEMBLE AND DECORATE BÛCHE DE NOËL:

1. When you are ready to frost the cake, unroll it very carefully, leaving it flat on the towel. Be sure frosting is at room temperature, well beaten and creamy. Use rubber scraper to spread frosting to cake edges, making a layer almost as thick as your finger. Save about ¾ cup (185 ml) frosting for outside of log.

2. Lift one end of the towel to help start the cake rolling. Roll cake onto the filling, jelly-roll style, but *without* the towel. Set rolled cake on platter, seam down. Cover cake sides (but not ends) with remaining frosting. Draw tines of fork through the frosting to make ridges.

3. To add chocolate bark: carefully stick chocolate curls on their sides in the frosting, or if using slivers stick their long edges into the frosting. Add mushrooms and leaves in groups as shown.

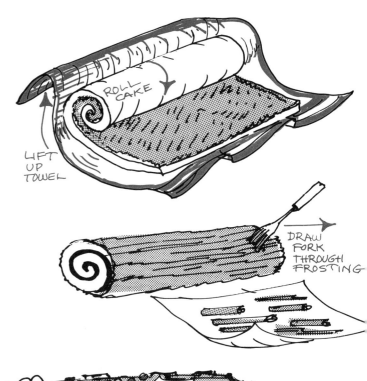

CRANBERRY BREAD *or* APRICOT BREAD

Sliced Cranberry bread is a festive treat served with tea *or* cocoa. You can also replace cranberries with apricots to make the Apricot Bread variation at the end of this recipe.

GIFT NOTE: To make three gifts instead of one, bake this recipe in 3 baby loaf pans. Or double the recipe to make 2 full loaves *or* 6 baby loaves. Wrapped airtight, Cranberry Bread may be baked ahead and frozen. To give, wrap loaves in plastic bags *or* plastic wrap and tie with ribbon and identifying tag. You can give the bread right in the baking pan for a double gift—and be sure to include the recipe.

EQUIPMENT:
Measuring cups and spoons
Sifter
2 mixing bowls
2 knives *or* pastry blender
Electric mixer *or* mixing spoon
Nut chopper *or* food processor *or*
    blender *or* cutting board and knife
Grater
Wax paper
Rubber scraper
Loaf pan 9″ × 5″ ×3″ (22 × 12.5 × 7.5
    cm) *or* 3 baby loaf pans 5¾″ × 3¼″
    × 2″ (14.5 × 8 × 5 cm)

FOODS YOU WILL NEED:
¼ cup (½ stick) margarine (60 ml; 60 g),
    plus extra for greasing pans
2 cups all-purpose flour (500 ml; 325 g)
1 cup granulated sugar (250 ml; 210 g)
1½ teaspoons baking powder (7.5 ml)
½ teaspoon baking soda (2.5 ml)
1 teaspoon salt (5 ml)
3 tablespoons wheat germ (45 ml)
1 orange
¾ cup orange juice (185 ml)
1 egg
½ cup walnuts (125 ml; 65 g)
2 cups fresh cranberries, washed (500
    ml, 240 g)

Ingredients:	How To:

Ingredients:

(To make one regular loaf or 3 baby loaves)

2 cups all-purpose flour (500 ml; 325 g)
1 cup granulated sugar (250 ml; 210 g)
1½ teaspoons baking powder (7.5 ml)
½ teaspoon baking soda (2.5 ml)
1 teaspoon salt (5 ml)
3 tablespoons wheat germ (45 ml)

¼ cup (½ stick) margarine (60 ml; 60 g)

PASTRY BLENDER

1 orange
¾ cup orange juice (185 ml)
1 egg

½ cup walnuts (125 ml; 65 g)
2 cups fresh cranberries, washed and picked over (500 ml; 240 g)

How To:

1. Grease pan(s) with margarine. Turn oven on to 350° F (175° C).

2. In one mixing bowl, sift flour, sugar, baking powder and soda, and salt. Add wheat germ.

3. Break margarine into small pieces and add to flour mixture. Use 2 knives that cut across each other *or* pastry blender to "cut in" shortening until it blends with flour and forms crumbly pieces the size of dry rice.

4. Grate peel of orange (but not the white part, which is bitter) on wax paper. Add peel to second mixing bowl. Add orange juice and egg and beat well.

5. Coarsely chop nuts, then cranberries, using nut chopper *or* blender *or* food processor *or* knife on cutting board. Set nuts and berries aside on wax paper.

6. Use rubber scraper to help scoop orange-egg mixture into the crumbly flour-shortening batter. Mix until well combined. Stir in nuts and cranberries.

7. Spoon batter into greased pan(s) and smooth top. Then spread batter away from center toward pan sides (to make center rise higher). Place pan in preheated 350°F (175° C)

2 cups dry apricots (500 ml; 300 g)
¾ cup apricot juice (185 ml)

APRICOT BREAD VARIATION: Follow recipe above *except* substitute apricots and apricot juice (prepared as follows) for cranberries and orange juice.

Measure apricots, then chop *or* cut them into small pieces. Cover them with water in a saucepan and set on stove. Cover with lid and bring water to a boil over high heat. Lower heat and simmer two minutes only.

oven and set timer to bake 60 minutes for large loaf, 35 to 45 minutes for baby loaf, or until bread is golden and toothpick set in center comes out clean. Cool 5 minutes, then remove bread from pan and cool on wire rack. (Or let cool right in pan.) Cranberry bread cuts most easily the day after it has been baked. Also try it toasted and buttered.

Set strainer over large measuring cup. Pour apricots into strainer. Use this fruit instead of berries in recipe. Measure liquid drained from apricots; you need ¾ cup (185 ml). Pour additional water over apricots in strainer if needed to make that amount. Use this juice instead of orange juice in recipe.

LEMON BREAD

This is a light, slightly tart quick bread textured with finely chopped walnuts.

GIFT NOTE: Bake ahead and freeze in plastic bags. One recipe makes three gift baby-size loaves; or you can double the recipe for more. Give with a new baking pan and the recipe attached.

EQUIPMENT:
3 baby loaf pans (6″ × 3½″ × 2″ [15 × 9 × 5 cm])
Measuring cups and spoons
Grater
Wax paper
Lemon squeezer
2 mixing bowls
Electric mixer *or* mixing spoon
Rubber scraper
Sifter
Nut chopper *or* blender *or* food processor
Cake tester *or* toothpick
Potholders
Table knife
Wire rack

FOODS YOU WILL NEED:
Bread:
2 lemons
6 tablespoons butter *or* margarine (90 g), at room temperature *plus* extra to grease pans
1 cup granulated sugar (250 ml; 210 g)
2 eggs
1½ cups all-purpose flour (375 ml; 245 g)
1 teaspoon baking powder (5 ml)
½ teaspoon salt (2.5 ml)
½ cup minus 2 tablespoons milk (220 ml)
1 cup shelled walnuts, chopped finely (250 ml; 125 g)
Lemon Glaze:
1 tablespoon lemon juice (15 ml)
½ cup confectioners' sugar (125 ml; 65 g)

Ingredients:

How To:

(To make 3 baby loaves)

2 lemons

1. Turn oven on to 350° F (175° C). Grate peel of lemons on wax paper (use only yellow part; do not grate white, as it is bitter). You need 2 teaspoons of peel. Cut both lemons and squeeze juice; remove seeds. You need 3 tablespoons (45 ml) juice. Set peel and juice aside.

2. Grease pans generously with butter *or* margarine. Set pans aside.

6 tablespoons butter *or* margarine (90 g), at room temperature

1 cup granulated sugar (250 ml; 210 g)

2 eggs

1½ cups all-purpose flour (375 ml; 245 g)

1 teaspoon baking powder (5 ml)

½ teaspoon salt (2.5 ml)

½ cup minus 2 tablespoons milk (220 ml)

1 cup shelled walnuts (250 ml; 125 g)

6. Use potholders to remove pans from oven and set on heat-proof surface. Cool cakes 5 minutes. Run a table knife between sides of each cake to separate it from its pan. Then tip cake out of pan and place right side up on wire rack. While still hot, coat cake tops with Lemon Glaze following. Let glaze harden before wrapping cakes.

LEMON GLAZE: Combine 1 tablespoon (15 ml) lemon juice with ½ cup (125 ml) sifted confectioners' sugar and beat until smooth. Spread on hot cakes.

3. In large mixing bowl, beat butter and sugar until smooth. Stir in grated lemon peel and 2 tablespoons (30 ml) lemon juice.

4. Break eggs into a measuring cup and remove any shells. Add eggs to butter-sugar batter and beat well.

Sift in flour, baking powder, and salt. Stir or beat slowly, adding milk a little at a time. Beat until smooth.

5. In nut chopper, blender, *or* food processor, chop nuts a few at a time, until fine. Stir nuts into batter.

Spoon batter into prepared pans, filling two-thirds full. Place pans in preheated 350° F (175° C) oven and set timer to bake 35 minutes, or until cake tester poked in center comes out clean.

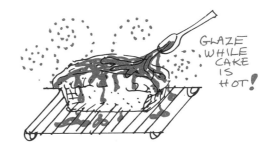

GLAZE WHILE CAKE IS HOT!

ORANGE HOLIDAY BREAD

The orange flavor gives this fruit-and-nut-filled yeast bread a delicious aroma. Shape it into braids, wreaths, or sculptured angels and top with Orange Sugar Glaze.

GIFT NOTE: Bake bread ahead, wrap in plastic bags, and freeze. To give as a gift, just tie a decorative bow on the plastic bag. Or, the bread and its recipe can be packaged with a bread-baking pan. Label: Orange Holiday Bread. Serve warm or toasted.

EQUIPMENT:
Bread:
Measuring cups and spoons
3 small bowls
Large mixing bowl
Wooden spoon
Grater
Wax paper
2 cookie sheets
Spatula
Ruler
Paring knife *or* scissors
Fork
Pastry brush
Timer
Wire rack

Orange Sugar Glaze:
Sifter
Mixing bowl
Whisk
Spoon

FOODS YOU WILL NEED:
Bread:
½ cup water (125 ml)
2 packages active dry yeast (½ ounce; 14 g) *or* equivalent amount of compressed yeast
½ cup granulated sugar (125 ml; 105 g)
Grated peel of 2 oranges (about 2 tablespoons, 30 ml)
1½ cups warm orange juice (375 ml)
2 tablespoons melted butter *or* oil (30 ml) *plus* extra oil for greasing pans and paper
2 teaspoons salt (10 ml)
¼ teaspoon ground cardamom (1.2 ml)
⅓ cup wheat germ (80 ml)
6 to 7 cups unbleached all-purpose flour (about 1 kg)

Optional flavoring
(use any or all of the following):
½ cup blanched slivered almonds *or* chopped hazelnuts *or* walnuts (125 ml; 67 g)
½ cup golden raisins (125 ml; 80 g)
½ cup pine nuts (125 ml; 160 g)
½ cup thinly sliced citron *or* chopped candied orange peel (125 ml)
1 egg

Orange Sugar Glaze:
1¼ cups confectioners' sugar, sifted (310 ml; 130 g)
3 tablespoons orange juice (45 ml) *or* hot milk
1 teaspoon vanilla extract (5 ml)
Candied cherries
Blanched almonds, whole *or* halved

Ingredients:

(To make 2 large braids or 2 sculptured angels)

½ cup warm water (125 ml)

2 packages active dry yeast (½ ounce; 14 g) or equivalent amount of compressed yeast

½ cup granulated sugar (125 ml; 105g)

2 oranges

1½ cups warm (not hot!) orange juice (375 ml)

2 tablespoons melted butter *or* oil (30 ml)

2 teaspoons salt (10 ml)

¼ teaspoon ground cardamom (1.2 ml)

⅓ cup wheat germ (80 ml)

3 cups unbleached all-purpose flour (750 ml; 500 g), plus extra as needed

How To:

YEAST

1. In small bowl, measure yeast into ½ cup *warm* water (not hot! or yeast, a living organism, will be killed). Measure ½ cup (125 ml) sugar. Take about 1 tablespoon sugar out of cup and add it to yeast-water. Stir. Set aside rest of sugar. Set aside yeast mixture until it "proves" and looks bubbly.

2. While yeast is proving, grate oranges (brightly colored peel only; white part tastes bitter) over wax paper.

3. In large mixing bowl, combine warm orange juice, melted butter *or* oil, salt, and sugar set aside in step 1 (½ cup minus 1 tablespoon). Mix well. Test temperature; when warm (not hot), stir in yeast mixture. Add grated orange peel, cardamom, wheat germ, and about 3 cups (750 ml) flour. Stir well and hard until dough feels stretchy and looks elastic as the gluten develops. Add additional flour, a cup at a time, until a dough ball forms.

4. Sprinkle flour on work surface and on hands. Turn dough out of bowl and knead by folding it over toward you then pushing it away while leaning on it with the heels of your hands. Give dough a quarter turn and repeat the folding and pushing. Add more flour as necessary. Knead until dough is no longer sticky, but looks satiny and smooth (about 5 minutes).

5. Wash and dry large mixing bowl. Grease it with some oil. Set dough ball in bowl, then turn dough over so its top is greased. Cover dough with piece of wax paper.

6. Dough must now rise for the first time. Set bowl in a warm place away from cold drafts. In cold weather you can place dough in oven (heat *off*!) with a pan of warm water beneath oven shelf. Let rise until double in size (about 1½ hours). Dough has risen enough when you poke two fingers into top and the depressions remain. When this

happens, it is time to PUNCH! down dough with your fist to knock some extra air bubbles out of the dough.

7. If you are adding any fruits and/or nuts to dough, measure them out into a small bowl now.
NOTE: Angels look prettiest made from smooth dough without nuts; braids are fine with nuts in dough. Again flour work surface and turn out dough. Press dough into a flat shape and sprinkle on fruits and nuts; knead dough until they are well worked in.

8. Turn oven on to 350° F (175° C). Divide dough in half. You can now shape plain round *or* oval loaves, and set them on greased cookie sheets to rise a second time, or shape braids *or* angels as described below.

Angels: Make one angel from each half of dough. Working with one piece first, divide it two thirds for body and one third for head, wings, arms, feet. Follow sketch to shape pieces. First form body into triangle, then mold other features. To attach one piece to another, brush joining point first with a little milk *or* beaten egg so they will stick. Hair can be a long thin braid *or* twist, or a series of skinny ropes shaped into curls. Brush face with egg *or* milk before adding simple dough features.

Set angels on greased cookie sheet. Dough must now rise a second time. For angels, this takes roughly 20 to 25 minutes; they should be almost, but not quite, double in size. After rising, brush them lightly with egg glaze: one egg beaten in bowl with fork. Bake in preheated 350° F (175° C) oven for about 30 minutes, or until golden and bread sounds hollow when tapped with your knuckle. Lift from sheet with spatula (or 2 spatulas) and cool on wire rack.

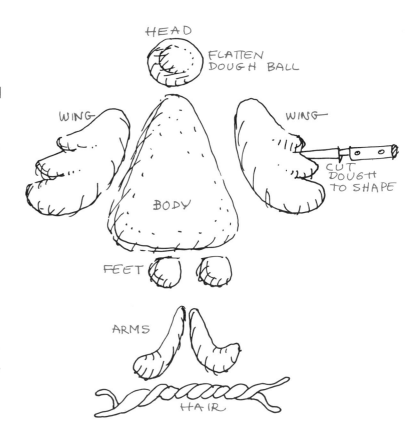

Remember dough will rise and all shapes will swell up. Add stripes *or* curved lines of dough on skirt. Repeat for second angel.

Braids: Make one large braid from each half of dough recipe. To braid, work with one half-recipe first. Divide it into three equal lumps. Roll each lump into a rope roughly 1″ × 20″ (2.5 × 51 cm) or longer. Place ropes side by side and pinch them together at one end. Hold this end with the heel of one hand while braiding the three lengths with your fingers as shown. Turn over each rope and pull it very slightly as you braid it. When complete, pinch ends together to hold and tuck under loaf. NOTE: For a wreath, pull braid slightly longer than usual and shape into a ring. Pinch ends together to hold.

Set braid *or* wreath on greased cookie sheet and cover with greased wax paper. Repeat for second braid. Let rise until *almost* double in size (about 1 hour).

Follow directions for angel to coat braid *or* wreath with egg glaze and bake. Set timer to bake 40 to 45 minutes, or until golden. Cool braid *or* wreath on wire rack. When thoroughly cold, coat with Orange Sugar Glaze.

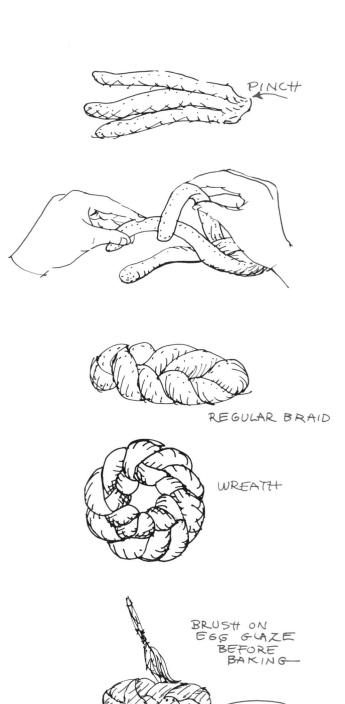

PINCH

REGULAR BRAID

WREATH

BRUSH ON EGG GLAZE BEFORE BAKING

ORANGE SUGAR GLAZE

Ingredients: **How To:**

(To make ⅔ cup [160 ml] frosting glaze)

1¼ cups confectioners' sugar, sifted (310 ml; 130 g)
3 tablespoons orange juice *or* hot milk (45 ml)
1 teaspoon vanilla extract (5 ml)
Candied cherries
Blanched almonds

1. In mixing bowl, combine and whisk sugar, juice *or* milk, and vanilla.

2. When smooth, dribble frosting from a spoon all over breads. For braids and wreaths, garnish by setting cherries and almonds into soft frosting. Allow frosting to harden before wrapping and freezing.

NANCY'S SPICED PECANS

Spiced nuts make a surprisingly different snack or hors d'oeuvre.

GIFT NOTE: Package nuts in an airtight container, or decorated coffee can.

EQUIPMENT:
Measuring cups and spoons
Jelly roll pan
Saucepan
Rubber scraper
2 wooden spoons

INGREDIENTS:
1 pound pecans, shelled and halved, *or* blanched almonds, halved *or* whole (450 g)
⅓ cup butter (80 ml; 80 g)
¼ cup granulated sugar (60 ml; 55 g)
Spices:
½ teaspoon cinnamon (2.5 ml)
½ teaspoon ground ginger (2.5 ml)
¼ teaspoon ground nutmeg (1.2 ml)
¼ teaspoon ground cardamom (1.2 ml)
⅛ teaspoon ground cloves (.5 ml)

Ingredients:

How To:

(To make 1 pound [450 g] nuts)

1 pound pecans, shelled and halved, *or* blanched almonds, halved *or* whole (450 g)
⅓ cup butter (80 ml; 80 g)
¼ cup granulated sugar (60 ml; 55 g)
Spices:
½ teaspoon (2.5 ml) *each*: cinnamon and ground ginger
¼ teaspoon (1.2 ml) *each*: ground nutmeg and cardamom
⅛ teaspoon ground cloves (.5ml)

1. Turn oven on to 300° F (150° C). Place nuts on jelly roll pan and set in preheated oven to roast for 15 minutes.

2. In saucepan, combine butter and sugar and set on stove over low heat. Stir with wooden spoon until butter melts. Then add spices and stir.

3. After 15 minutes, remove nuts from oven and set pan on heat-proof surface. Pour butter-spice mixture over nuts. Stir nuts and sauce together with 2 wooden spoons until all nuts are coated. Return pan to 300° F (150° C) oven and set timer to bake 30 minutes. After baking, let nuts cool in pan.

TOASTED COCONUT CHIPS

Toasted fresh coconut, lightly salted, makes a delicious and irresistible snack. Bet you can't eat just one!

GIFT NOTE: Coconut chips can be made ahead, as they keep well when stored airtight in a dry place. Pack them in attractive glass jars and give with a copy of the recipe. Label: "Toasted Coconut Chips. Serve as snack or hors d'oeuvre."

EQUIPMENT:
Screwdriver
Hammer
Bowl
Roasting pan *or* jelly roll pan
Vegetable peeler
Measuring cups and spoons
Jars

FOODS YOU WILL NEED:
1 fresh coconut
Salt, to taste

How To:

(To make about 1 quart [1 liter])

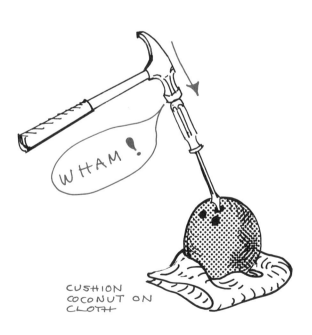

WHAM!

CUSHION COCONUT ON CLOTH

1. Turn oven on to 350° F (175° C).
   Ask an adult to help you pierce eyes of coconut with screwdriver and hammer. Drain coconut milk into bowl and save to drink (strain if needed).

2. Set drained coconut on roasting pan and place in preheated oven. Set timer to roast 30 minutes, or until shell cracks in a couple of places. Then remove coconut from oven and lower heat to 300° F (150° C).

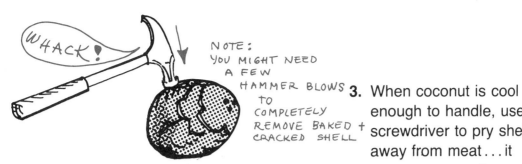

3. When coconut is cool enough to handle, use screwdriver to pry shell away from meat...it comes away quite easily. Keep meat in large pieces. Discard shell. Use vegetable peeler to peel off brown skin and discard.

Use peeler to slice chips from edges of coconut meat as shown. Spread chips in a single layer on roasting pan. Sprinkle chips lightly with salt. Note: With adult help, you can also peel chips with thin slicing disk of food processor.

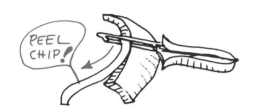

4. Place pan in 300° F (150° C) oven and set timer for 25 minutes but check occasionally and bake *only* until chips are a light golden color and crisp.

Remove from oven and cool. Add more salt, to taste, if needed. Pack loosely in clean dry jars with lids.

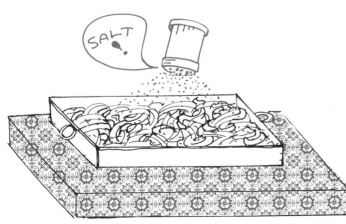

CHEESE MATCHSTICKS

The tips of these crisp cheese pastry sticks are dipped in paprika to make them look like matchsticks.

GIFT NOTE: Package in airtight container to retain crispness. Label: "Savory" Cheese Matchsticks. Serve with soup or as hors d'oeuvres.

EQUIPMENT:
Measuring cups and spoons
Sifter
Large mixing bowl
Pastry blender *or* fork
Grater and wax paper *or* food processor
Rolling pin
Knife
Ruler
Cookie sheet
Timer
Small bowl

FOODS YOU WILL NEED:
1½ cups all-purpose flour (375 ml; 245 g)
1 teaspoon salt (5 ml)
¼ teaspoon cayenne powder (1.2 ml)
½ cup (1 stick) margarine *or* butter (125 ml; 120 g), at room temperature
1½ cups sharp Cheddar cheese, grated (375 ml; 75 g)
3 to 4 tablespoons ice water (45 to 60 ml)
¼ cup paprika, medium or mild-type (60 ml)

Ingredients:

How To:

(To make about 60 sticks)

1½ cups all-purpose flour (375 ml; 245 g)
1 teaspoon salt (5 ml)
¼ teaspoon cayenne powder (1.2 ml)
½ cup (1 stick) margarine *or* butter (125 ml; 120 g), at room temperature

1. Turn oven on to 425° F (220° C). Sift flour and salt into mixing bowl. Add cayenne. Cut up margarine *or* butter into bits and add to flour, working it in with fork *or* pastry blender until mixture is crumbly.

1 ½ cups sharp Cheddar cheese (375 ml; 75 g)
3 to 4 tablespoons ice water (45 to 60 ml)

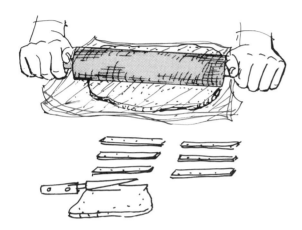

¼ cup paprika (60 ml)

2. Grate cheese using grater over wax paper *or* in food processor. Add cheese and ice water to dough and stir until mixture forms a ball.

3. Roll out dough about ¼″ (.5 cm) thick on lightly floured surface. Cut dough with knife into sticks about the size of your middle finger. Set sticks on ungreased cookie sheet and place in 425° F (220° C) oven. Set timer to bake 15 minutes, or until sticks are golden.

4. Measure ¼ cup (60 ml) paprika into small bowl. After baking, let sticks cool on sheet until you can touch them comfortably. Then pick up each stick and dip one end into paprika. Store sticks in airtight container.

PRETZELS

For a perfect snack, try these chewy pretzels, sprinkled with coarse salt. You may not want to give them away!

GIFT NOTE: Pretzels can be baked ahead and frozen in plastic bags. To give, leave in plastic bags but set in decorative cannisters or napkin-lined baskets.

EQUIPMENT:
Small and large mixing bowls
Measuring cups and spoons
4-cup measure (1 liter)
Mixing spoon
2 teacups
Fork
Ruler
Cookie sheet
Pastry brush
Timer
Wire rack
Spatula

FOODS YOU WILL NEED:
1 package active dry yeast (¼ ounce; 7 g) *or* equivalent amount compressed yeast
¼ plus ¾ cup warm water (250 ml)
1 tablespoon granulated sugar (15 ml)
Margarine for greasing baking pan
1 egg
¼ cup Kosher salt *or* other coarse-crystal salt (60 ml)
4 cups all-purpose flour (1 liter; 665 g)
1 teaspoon salt (5 ml)

Ingredients:

How To:

(To make about 24 pretzels)

1 package active dry yeast (¼ ounce; 7 g) *or* compressed yeast
¼ cup warm (not hot!) water (60 ml)
1 tablespoon granulated sugar (15 ml)

1. In one small bowl, combine yeast, ¼ cup *warm* water (if too hot, water will kill yeast!), and sugar. Stir once, then let mixture sit about 5 minutes until yeast proves and looks bubbly.

1 egg
¼ cup Kosher salt (60 ml)

2. In one teacup, beat egg with fork. Set egg aside. Measure salt into second teacup and set it aside.

4 cups all-purpose flour (1 liter; 665 g)

3. Measure flour into largest (4-cup, 1 liter) measuring cup and set it aside.

¾ cup *warm* water (185 ml)
1 teaspoon salt (5 ml)

4. In large mixing bowl, combine ¾ cup (185 ml) *warm* water and salt. Stir

until you are sure water is comfortably warm, not hot. Then add bubbly yeast mixture. Stir in 2½ cups of flour (625 ml; 405 g). Add more flour if necessary until dough forms a ball. Place dough on floured work surface.

5. Knead dough about 5 minutes by folding it and pushing it away from you with the heels of your hands. When done, dough should no longer feel sticky and should form a satin-smooth ball.

6. Turn oven on to 425° F (220°C). Divide dough ball in half. Divide each half into 12 equal-sized balls. Roll each ball into a rope about 12″ (30.5 cm) long and the thickness of your finger. Shape pretzels on floured work surface:

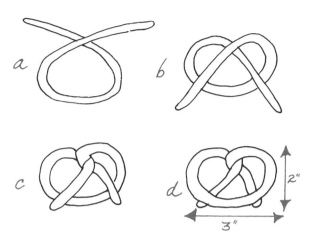

(a) Form one 12″ (30.5 cm) rope into a loop. Cross legs of loop at top. (b) Then bring crossed legs down over the center of loop. (c) Twist legs once. (d) Tuck leg tips under loop.

Lift formed pretzels onto greased cookie sheet. Neaten shapes into 3″ (7.5 cm) wide ovals about 2″ (5 cm) high. Brush pretzels with beaten egg and sprinkle with Kosher salt.

7. Place cookie sheet in preheated 425° F (220° C) oven and set timer to bake 12 to 15 minutes, or until pretzels are golden. Remove sheet from oven. Lift hot pretzels from sheet with spatula and cool on wire rack.

Sauces,
Cheese,
Condiments,
etc.

CHOCOLATE SUNDAE SAUCE

This rich fudge sauce is delicious served warm or cold over pound cake or ice cream.

GIFT NOTE: Package sauce in half-pint jelly jars with screw-on lids. Label: "Chocolate Sundae Sauce. Refrigerate. Serve warm or cold over ice cream."

EQUIPMENT:
Measuring cups and spoons
Small saucepan
Wooden spoon
Rubber scraper
Jar with lid

FOODS YOU WILL NEED:
2 squares Baker's unsweetened chocolate (2 ounces; 50 g)
8 tablespoons water (120 ml)
6 to 8 tablespoons sugar (90 to 120 ml)
2 tablespoons butter (30 ml)
½ teaspoon vanilla extract (2.5 ml)

Ingredients:

How To:

(To make 1 cup; 250 ml)

2 squares Baker's unsweetened chocolate (2 ounces; 50 g)
8 tablespoons water (120 ml)
6 to 8 tablespoons sugar (90 to 120 ml), to taste

2 tablespoons butter (30 ml)
½ teaspoon vanilla extract (2.5 ml)

1. In small saucepan, combine chocolate, water, and sugar. Set on stove over low heat and stir constantly until chocolate melts and mixture is blended smoothly.

2. Stir in butter and vanilla, mixing until butter melts. Cool and store in covered jar. Refrigerate.

VARIATIONS: Instead of vanilla extract, you can substitute 1 teaspoon (5 ml) instant coffee powder or ½ teaspoon (2.5 ml) almond *or* orange *or* rum extract.

PANCAKE SYRUPS

Instead of maple syrup on your pancakes, try these easy-to-make sauces with fresh tangy flavors.

GIFT NOTE: Pack the syrup in half-pint jelly jars with screw-on lids. Label: "Orange (or Raspberry) Syrup. Refrigerate. Serve on pancakes, waffles, or ice cream."

EQUIPMENT:
Measuring cups and spoons
Wax paper
2 mixing bowls
Rubber scraper
½-pint jars with lids
Grater (for orange)
For Raspberry Syrup:
    Blender *or* food processor
    Strainer and spoon

FOODS YOU WILL NEED:
Light corn syrup
Lemon juice
Orange Syrup:
    1 whole orange
    1 small can frozen orange juice
    concentrate (6 ounces; 177 ml), at
    room temperature
Raspberry Syrup:
    1 box frozen whole raspberries, (10
    ounces; 283 g), defrosted *or* 1 pint
    fresh, washed raspberries

ORANGE SYRUP

Ingredients:

(To make about 1½ cups; 375 ml)

1 whole orange

10 tablespoons frozen orange juice concentrate (150 ml)
4 teaspoons lemon juice (60 ml)
1 cup light corn syrup (250 ml)

How To:

1. Grate orange peel on wax paper. Don't grate white part of peel, as it is bitter. Scrape peel into bowl.

2. Add orange juice concentrate right from can, along with lemon juice and corn syrup. Stir. Pack in jar with lid. Store in refrigerator.

RASPBERRY SYRUP

Ingredients: **How To:**

(To make about 1 cup; 250 ml)

1 box frozen whole raspberries, defrosted (10 ounces;
283 g) *or* 1 pint fresh, washed
raspberries

1. If using frozen berries, set
   them in a strainer over a
   bowl and drain well. Save
   juice for another purpose.
   Put fresh *or* drained frozen
   berries into blender *or*
   food processor and purée.
   Measure 8 tablespoons of
   purée (120 ml) into a bowl.

1 cup light corn syrup (250 ml)
2 teaspoons *or* more lemon
juice (30 ml), to taste

2. Stir in corn syrup and
   lemon juice. Pack in jar
   with lid and refrigerate.

HOMEMADE YOGURT CHEESE

You will be surprised how easy it is to make a creamy, mild cheese simply by draining the water from plain yogurt. The flavor and consistency of this cheese are similar to that of French *Boursin*, and, like it, can be flavored with herbs *or* spices.

GIFT NOTE: Pack the cheese in a pottery crock *or* covered glass jar, and refrigerate. Label: "Homemade Yogurt Cheese Spread (Herb Flavored—or other flavor). Refrigerate."

EQUIPMENT:
Mixing bowl
Measuring cups and spoons
Large spoon
12" (30.5 cm) square piece of double-thickness cheesecloth
Plate or wax paper
14" (35 cm) length of string
Hanging hook *or* nail—optional
Crock *or* jar, with lid

FOODS YOU WILL NEED:
1 cup *plain* yogurt (8 ounces; 250 ml)
¼ teaspoon salt (1.2 ml)
Optional Flavoring:
Curry powder
or black pepper, freshly cracked
or Herb Blend: pepper, onion powder, dill, thyme, basil (*or* oregano
or paprika
or toasted sesame seeds
or poppy seeds
or finely chopped walnuts

Ingredients:

How To:

(To make about ¾ cup cheese [185 ml])

1 cup *plain* yogurt (8 ounces; 250 ml)

¼ teaspoon salt (1.2 ml)

1. First stir yogurt and salt together in mixing bowl. For plain cheese, go on to Step 2. If you want extra flavoring, add herbs *or* spices now.

   Add any *one* of separate flavorings in Foods You Will Need list (amounts to taste) *or*, for *Curried Cheese:* ¾ teaspoon curry powder (4 ml); for *Herb Blend:* ⅛ teaspoon freshly ground black pepper (.5 ml), a pinch of onion powder, and ¼ teaspoon (1.2 ml) *each* of dry dill, thyme, and basil *or* oregano.

2. Arrange cheesecloth, double-thick, flat on top of a plate *or* piece of wax paper. Spoon yogurt mixture onto center of cloth.

3. Gather up all edges of cheesecloth, twist into a pouch, and tie neck closed with string. Tie loose ends of string into a hanging loop as shown.

4. Hang yogurt from a hook, nail, *or* from the neck of the faucet in the kitchen sink. Put a bowl directly under pouch to catch drips. (Don't turn water on if yogurt hangs in sink!)

NOTE: To increase recipe to make 2½ cups cheese (625 ml) use 2 quarts plain yogurt (2 liters) plus ½ teaspoon salt (2.5 ml).

5. Hang yogurt overnight—at least 12 hours—or longer, until *all* water stops dripping out. At this point, cheese is done. Unwrap cheesecloth. Pack cheese in covered crock. Or form into ball and roll in seasoning.

6. If you like, you can coat the top of the cheese, in the crock, by pressing on some freshly cracked pepper *or* paprika *or* toasted sesame seeds *or* poppy seeds *or* chopped nuts. Close crock and refrigerate. Serve on crackers.

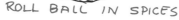

ROLL BALL IN SPICES   OR PACK IN A CROCK

VANILLA SUGAR

Vanilla-flavored sugar is the easiest of all gifts to make. Give it to the gourmet cooks on your list.

GIFT NOTE: Package sugar in decorative glass jars *or* bottles with tight lids. Label: "Vanilla Sugar. Use for baking."

EQUIPMENT:
Clean, dry, attractively shaped glass jars *or* spice jars with lids
Measuring cup
Paring knife

FOODS YOU WILL NEED:
Granulated *or* confectioners' sugar
Whole vanilla beans (found on specialty shelf of grocery store or in gourmet shops)

How To:

Select vanilla beans that are pliable and fragrant, not stiff and dried out. Fill jar with sugar, add vanilla bean (whole *or* piece) and close jar. Label your jar.

Use one whole bean for 3 to 5 pounds (1.5 to 2.5 kg) of sugar. Use a half *or* quarter of a bean for a smaller jar. Bean can be reused until it is dried out; simply replace sugar in container.

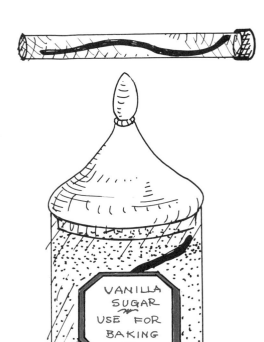

CRANBERRY-ORANGE RELISH

This no-cook relish is easy to make and tastes much better than canned cranberry sauce served with your holiday turkey *or* goose. The flavor improves on standing in the refrigerator, so make the relish a few days ahead. Relish may also be frozen.

GIFT NOTE: Pack in recycled peanut butter *or* jelly jars with screw-type lids, or use canning jars. Label: "Cranberry-Orange Relish. Refrigerate. Serve cold with roasted poultry or meat."

EQUIPMENT:
Colander
Measuring cups and spoons
Blender *or* food processor *or* meat
   grinder with coarse blade
Mixing bowl
Spoon
Clean, dry glass jars with lids

FOODS YOU WILL NEED:
4 cups whole fresh cranberries (1 liter;
   480 g)
1 orange
1 apple
½ cup fresh *or* canned (drained)
   pineapple pieces (125 ml)—optional
2 cups granulated sugar (500 ml; 420 g),
   to taste
½ teaspoon ground ginger (2.5 ml)
½ teaspoon nutmeg (2.5 ml)

How to:

(To make about 1 quart [1 liter] relish)

1. Wash cranberries in colander. Discard spoiled berries and any stems. Coarsely chop cranberries in blender—½ cup at a time—(do not purée) *or* use food processor (for a second only) *or* put through meat grinder. Put chopped berries in bowl.

2. Wash orange and apple and cut them into quarters. Remove seeds. Cut fruit into smaller pieces. Chop *or* grind orange and apple (pulp and peel) as you did berries. Add chopped fruit to bowl. Chop and add pineapple if you have it. Add sugar and spices and stir well.

3. Spoon relish into jars, wipe jars clean, and cover with lids. Label. Store in refrigerator.

APRICOT-PINEAPPLE MARMALADE

One recipe makes nine gift jars of marmalade at one time! Cooked without adding artificial pectin, this slightly tart fruit-filled marmalade is special enough to use either as a spread for Christmas breakfast toast or as a sauce on a yuletide party soufflé.

GIFT NOTE: If you like, you can use self-sealing jelly jars; sterilize and seal them according to jar manufacturer's directions. Properly sealed jars (unopened) can be stored in a cupboard and will last many months. Or use boiled (see step 5) jars with screw-on lids that are *not* sealed. Unsealed jars must be refrigerated or the marmalade will spoil. *Be absolutely sure to label jars*: Either "Apricot-Pineapple Marmalade. Sealed. Christmas (date)" *or* "Apricot-Pineapple Marmalade. Not Sealed. Store in refrigerator. (date)."

EQUIPMENT:
Measuring cups and spoons
Wax paper
Blender *or* food processor *or* knife and
   cutting board
Dutch oven *or* extra-large saucepan with
   lid
Grater
Lemon squeezer
Can opener
Wooden spoon
9 half-pint jelly jars with lids (self-sealing
   or recycled screw-on type)
Dishtowel
Tray
Paper towels
Rubber gloves *or* tongs

FOODS YOU WILL NEED:
1 pound dried apricot halves
   (440 g; 3 cups)
½ cup seedless raisins (125 ml; 110 g)
3 cups water (750 ml)
2 lemons (rind and juice)
1 can crushed pineapple (1 pound 4
   ounces; 567 g)
4 cups granulated sugar (1 liter; 840 g)
1 teaspoon ground ginger (5 ml)
½ teaspoon cinnamon (2.5 ml)

Ingredients: How To:

(To make 9 half-pint jars)

1 pound dried apricot halves
   440 g; 3 cups)
½ cup seedless raisins (125
   ml; 110 g)
3 cups water (750 ml)

1. Measure apricots onto a
   piece of wax paper. Pick
   over apricots and remove
   any pit fragments or
   stems. Apricots must be
   coarsely chopped (into
   pieces about the size of
   your smallest fingernail)

2 lemons

1 can crushed pineapple (1 pound 4 ounces; 567 g)

4 cups granulated sugar (1 liter; 840 g)

using the blender—chop ½ cup at a time—*or* the food processor *or* a knife and cutting board. Put all pieces into the Dutch oven *or* largest saucepan. Add raisins and water. Cover pot, set on stove over high heat, and bring to boil. Then lower heat and simmer 10 minutes.

2. Grate both lemons over wax paper. Then cut lemons in half and squeeze juice in squeezer; remove pits. Open can of pineapple. After apricots have simmered 10 minutes, add lemon peel and juice, pineapple, and sugar to pot. Stir with wooden spoon until sugar dissolves.

Leave lid off pot. Raise heat under pot, bring mixture to boil, then lower heat and boil very gently about 50 minutes, or until marmalade is not at all watery. It should be very thick and almost able to coat the wooden spoon. Stir occasionally while cooking. Lower heat if it starts to burn, or if fruit sticks too much.

3. While marmalade cooks, prepare jars. Whatever type of jars you use, they should be washed thoroughly with soap and hot water, then sterilized by putting them through the full dishwasher cycle *or* by setting them gently into a large pot, covering with water, and boiling gently about 20 minutes.

   Ask an adult to remove hot jars from boiling water with insulated rubber gloves or rubber-tipped tongs. Set clean jars on a dishtowel-lined tray. Just before using, replace dishtowel with sheet of wax paper (to catch spills).

1 teaspoon ground ginger (5 ml)
½ teaspoon cinnamon (2.5 ml)

4. When marmalade is thick enough, remove it from heat. Set pot on heat-proof surface and stir in ginger and cinnamon.

5. Spoon marmalade into clean hot jars. Fill almost to the top. Wipe spills off jar lip with damp (not dripping) paper towel. Screw on regular lids *or* self-sealing lids following manufacturer's directions. Let jars stand until cold. Wipe jars clean. Label.

SEASONED RICE MIXES

This is one of the easiest gifts from your kitchen—just assemble the dry ingredients for whichever flavor you prefer and package.

GIFT NOTE: Pack mix in an attractive airtight jar *or* tin and label with cooking directions: "Herb (or Curried) Rice Blend. Combine all rice mixture with 2 cups (500 ml) cold water and 1 tablespoon (15 ml) butter in saucepan. Cover. Bring to boil, reduce heat to low. Stir once with fork. Cover and simmer about 14 to 20 minutes, or until all liquid is absorbed. Serves 4 to 6."

EQUIPMENT:
Measuring cups and spoons
Bowl
Airtight jar *or* tin

INGREDIENTS:
Herb Rice:
1 cup uncooked rice (250 ml; 200 g)
2 beef bouillon cubes *or* equivalent
   powdered bouillon
½ teaspoon salt (2.5 ml)
½ teaspoon (2.5 ml) *each*: dried
   rosemary, marjoram, and thyme
   leaves
1 teaspoon dried green onion flakes (5
   ml)
Curried Rice:
1 cup uncooked rice (250 ml; 200 g)
2 chicken bouillon cubes *or* powdered
   bouillon
1½ teaspoons curry powder (7.5 ml)
¼ teaspoon ground cumin (1.2 ml)
1 teaspoon dry instant minced onion (5
   ml)
½ teaspoon *each* (2.5 ml): salt and dried
   parsley flakes.

Index

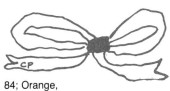

ABOUT THE AUTHOR

Susan Purdy has written and illustrated over twenty books for young readers, most of them in various craft fields. Her *Christmas Decorations for You to Make* has become a classic in the field. She has had innumerable articles published in *Ladies' Home Journal, Family Circle,* and *Good Housekeeping.*

Her career as a cooking teacher began with small gourmet cooking classes for children from ages seven to twelve. She also appeared on the CBS-TV *Patchwork Family* show for three years as its cooking specialist, and she is currently teaching cooking to young people at her daughter's Montessori school. In addition, she teaches adults as well as children at the Silo Cooking School in New Milford, Connecticut.